THE PAJAMA GAME

A Musical Comedy

Based on the novel " *Seven-and-a-Half Cents* "
by Richard Bissell

Music and Lyrics by

RICHARD ADLER and JERRY ROSS

Book by

GEORGE ABBOTT and RICHARD BISSELL

Scenery and Costumes by LEMUEL AYERS
Choreography by BOB FOSSE
Musical Direction by ROBERT LOWE
Orchestrations by DON WALKER
Dance Music Arrangements by ROGER ADAMS

American Production
Directed by GEORGE ABBOTT and JEROME ROBBINS
Reproduced by ROBERT E. GRIFFITH
Production Supervised by JEROME WHYTE

MUSIC

ACT ONE

OVERTURE
1. THE PAJAMA GAME—Opening
2. RACING WITH THE CLOCK
3. A NEW TOWN IS A BLUE TOWN
4. RACING WITH THE CLOCK—Reprise
5. I'M NOT AT ALL IN LOVE
6. I'M NOT AT ALL IN LOVE—Change
7. I'LL NEVER BE JEALOUS AGAIN
8. INTRODUCTION TO " HEY THERE "
8a. HEY THERE
9. HER IS (Verse)
9a. HER IS (Chorus)
9b. HER IS (Dance)
9c. SLEEP TITE
10. ONCE-A-YEAR DAY (and Polka)
10a. ONCE-A-YEAR DAY—Crossover
11. HER IS—REPRISE
12. SMALL TALK
12a. I'M NOT AT ALL IN LOVE—Incidental
13. THERE ONCE WAS A MAN (I Love You More)
14. FACTORY MUSIC
14a. SLOW DOWN
14b. FACTORY MUSIC
15. FINALE ACT I (Hey There)

ACT TWO

16. ENTR'ACTE
16a. OPENING ACT II
17. STEAM HEAT
17a. SMALL TALK—Incidental
18. HEY THERE—Reprise
18a. FACTORY MUSIC
19. THINK OF THE TIME I SAVE
20. HERNANDO'S HIDEAWAY
20a. HERNANDO'S HIDEAWAY DANCE
20b. HERNANDO'S HIDEAWAY DANCE—Incidental
21. I'LL NEVER BE JEALOUS AGAIN—Ballet (Part I)
21a. I'LL NEVER BE JEALOUS AGAIN—Ballet (Part II)
22. HEY THERE—Incidental
23. SEVEN-AND-A-HALF CENTS
23a. RUSH MUSIC
24. THERE ONCE WAS A MAN (I Love You More)—Reprise
25. THE PAJAMA GAME—Closing
25a. SEVEN-AND-A-HALF CENTS—Reprise

THE PAJAMA GAME

THE PAJAMA GAME was first presented at the St. James Theatre, New York City, on 13th May, 1954, *and at the Coliseum, London, on* 13th October, 1955

CHARACTERS (in order of appearance)

HINES
PREZ
JOE
HASLER
SID SOROKIN
GLADYS
MABEL
1st HELPER
2nd HELPER
CHARLIE
BABE WILLIAMS
MAE
BRENDA
POOPSIE
SALESMAN
POP
DANCERS and SINGERS

SCENES

ACT I

Scene 1.	Sewing Room of the Sleep Tite Pajama Factory.
Scene 2.	The same.
Scene 3.	A Hallway in the Factory.
Scene 4.	The Office.
Scene 5.	On the way to the Union Picnic.
Scene 6.	Picnic Grounds.
Scene 7.	Picnic Path.
Scene 8.	The Kitchen of Babe's House.
Scene 9.	A Hallway in the Factory.
Scene 10.	The Shop.

ACT II

Scene 1.	Eagle Hall.
Scene 2.	The Kitchen of Babe's House.
Scene 3.	A Hallway in the Factory.
Scene 4.	The Office.
Scene 5.	Hernando's Hideaway.
Scene 6.	Morning in the Office.
Scene 7.	A Street near the Park, followed by Hernando's Hideaway

PLACE: The action takes place in a small town in the Middle West.

TIME: The present.

Pre-Set	*House Tabs In. Traveller closed. Black Drop in. Scene 1, Lighting on 1. Bat. Pilots off.*
1 min. before Overture	*Send M.D. in.*
Start of Overture	*3 Bar-bells, Secondarys off. Check following: Factory set,* GIRLS *on stage, panels clear,* HINES *stage* R.
Overture	*" Seven-and-a-Half Cents," " Hey There," " Tick Tock," " I'm Not at all in Love," Hernando's Hideaway," " Small Talk," " Once-a-Year-Day ".*
End of " Small Talk " in Overture	*House lights out, Pilots out.* Warn Cue 2, 2a, 3, Flys, Traveller.
End of Overture—Applause	*House Tabs up.*

SCENE 1.

> HINES *enters from* R. *dancing to musical vamp. Crosses to* C. *and raises his hat.*

Music No. 1. " THE PAJAMA GAME " *Opening*

HINES. **This is a very serious drama. It's kind of a problem play. It's about Capital and Labour. I wouldn't bother to make such a point of all this except later on if you happen to** [*Crosses* R.C.] **see a lot of naked women being chased through the woods, I don't want you to get the wrong impression.** [C.] **This play is full of SYMBOLISM.**

Lighting Cue 2

I work in the Sleep Tite Pajama Factory in Cedar Rapids, Iowa.
[*He dances—Strut. Crosses* R.C. *He sings.*]
>   **The Pajama Game,**
>   **Is the game I'm in.**
>   **And I'm proud to be** [*Crosses* C.]
>   **In the Pajama Game**
>   **I love it.**
>   **I can hardly wait to wake** [R.C.]
>   **And get to work at eight**
>   **Nothing's quite the same as the Pajama Game** [C.]

[*Crosses* L.C. *Speaks.*] **I'm an EXECUTIVE.**

Cue 2a.

I'm a Time Study Man. I can tell you per second exactly how many stitches go into a pair of pajamas.

Black Drop away.

I can . . . time anything. You'll see when we get down to the factory.
[*Crosses far* R. *Takes out watch.*] **Let her go!**

Cue 3. Traveller open (Fast).

ACT I—SCENE 2. THE FACTORY

> *When the lights come on we see the* GIRLS *busy at work in the Factory.* D.R. *is a heap of cartons, rolls and bales of cloth, where a group of* GIRLS *are working.*
> U.S.C. *are more cartons and bales and rolls of cloth lying against the Factory wall which has three windows in it.*
> D.S. *and extending from* C. *stage off* L. *to the wings is a long bench on which are twelve sewing machines, bobbins of thread, and numerous pieces of material. There are six high stools* U.S. *of the bench, and six chairs* D.S. *of the bench. Some of the* GIRLS *are sitting at the bench. Above the bench are twelve shaded lamps, and hanging from the ceiling is an electric power cable which is connected to the* R. *end of the bench.*
> HINES *is* D.R. *and when Traveller is open he looks at his watch and stamps his foot. He crosses* U.C. *to* R. *of machines.*

Music No. 1 (Continued)

HINES. **All right girls. Hurry up! I've got my stop watch on you.** [*Stamps foot, then crosses* D.C. *putting his watch away.*] **Now watch for the symbolism.** [*He looks off* L.] **Ah-huh, here comes the President of the Union. Boy, is he sharp! He knows what's going on around here.**

> HINES *crosses to* D.L. PREZ *enters from* D.L., *crosses to* C., *speaks to* GIRLS *at machines.*

PREZ. **Hey, I lost my lunch bucket. Anybody seen my lunch bucket?**
HINES. **I told you he was sharp.**

PREZ crosses to stage R. where GIRLS are standing working by the window D.R. He goes up behind them and tickles GIRL, who giggles loudly.

PREZ. [*To* GIRL].   **Her is the cutest one.**

HINES [*To audience*].   **He's just relaxing, but there's another side to his character.**

JOE, a factory worker, enters D.R. and crosses in to D.R.

JOE.   **How about it, Prez?**

PREZ. [*Crossing to* L. *of* JOE].   **If we don't get a seven-and-a-half cent raise by the first of the month, we strike!**

JOE.   **You said it!**

PREZ.   **You said it!**

Both nod heads sharply, then exit D.R.

HINES [*Crossing back to* R.].   **See how ideas keep creeping through. That takes the sting off the sexy parts.** [*Stops* C., *looks off* U.R.]   **Oh, look out. Here comes my boss, Mr. Hasler.** [*Crosses to* R.C.]   **There's capital for you. Capital with a Capital C. He's a great economist.**

HASLER enters from U.R., crosses to GIRL at machine. Picks up scrap of material from carton R. of bench, throws it on bench, saying:

HASLER.   **Waste, waste, waste!!!**

GIRL dissolves into tears. HASLER crosses D.C. 2ND HELPER enters D.L. and crosses to HASLER. HASLER shouts at him.

Turn off those damn lights. [2ND HELPER *turns and runs off* D.L. HASLER *crosses* D.C. *and says to audience*.]   **Do you think J. P. Morgan got rich leaving lights burning all over Wall Street?** [*Looking* R.]   **Where's my secretary?** [*Looking* L.]   **Gladys!**

GLADYS enters from U.R. Crosses down o R. of HASLER.

GLADYS.   **Yes, Mr. Hasler?**

HINES [*Crosses back to* GLADYS].   **I love her, I love her.**

HASLER.   **Where's the new superintendent?**

GLADYS.   **We can't find him.** [*Looks off* L.]   **Here's Mabel . . . she'll know.**

MABEL enters from D.L. Crosses to L. of HASLER.

HASLER.   **Where's Sorokin?**

MABEL.   **He's around the plant somewhere, Mr. Hasler. First there was a leak in the water tower . . . then he went down to the boiler room.**

HASLER.   **Well, go find him.**

MABEL.   **Yes, Mr. Hasler.**

MABEL exits U.R.

HASLER.   **Gladys. Take a letter.**

GLADYS.   **Yes, sir.**

HASLER [*Crosses* L, *followed by* GLADYS].   **Board of Directors: Employees' demand for seven-and-a-half cents raise, absolutely unnecessary.** [*To* HINES.]   **Hines!**

HINES.   **Yes sir!**

HASLER.   **Keep things going.**

HINES.   **Okay, chief.**

(*Music No. 1 finishes*).

Music No. 2.   " RACING WITH THE CLOCK "

HASLER and GLADYS exit D.L. As they exit, HASLER continues dictation. HINES has crossed to stage C. by the machines and takes out his watch, then stamps his foot.

Hurry up, girls. Can't waste time. [*Crossing* D.L.]   **I've got my stop watch on you. Hurry up! Hurry up!**

HINES exits D.L.

GIRLS I [*Singing*].   **Hurry up, hurry up, hurry up, hurry up** [*etc.*]

GIRLS II.   **Can't waste time, can't waste time,**
                             When you're racing with the clock
                             When you're racing with the clock
                             And the second hand doesn't understand
                             That your back may break and your fingers ache
                             And your constitution isn't made of rock
                             It's a losing race when you're racing with the,
                             Racing with the,
                             Racing with the clock.

GIRLS I.   **It's a losing race when you're racing with the,**
                             Racing with the,
                             Racing with the clock.

HINES enters from D.L., crosses to D.R., and exits, saying as he goes:

HINES.   Hurry up, girls. Seconds are ticking. Seconds are ticking. Hurry up.

JOE pushes trolley from D.R. across stage to exit D.L.

GIRLS I.   Hurry up, hurry up,
Can't waste time, can't waste time

GIRLS II.   Hurry up, hurry up

GIRLS I.   Can't waste time, can't waste time

GIRLS II.   When you're racing with the clock
When you're racing with the clock

GIRLS I.   Can't waste time, can't waste time

GIRLS II.   And the second hand doesn't understand
That your back may break and your fingers ache

ALL GIRLS.   And your constitution isn't made of rock

GIRLS II.   It's a losing race when you're racing with the,
Racing with the,
Racing with the clock.

GIRLS I.   Can't waste time, can't waste time.

SINGING BOY I [*Crosses L. to C. joined by* GIRL. *who crosses from group* R. *Sings.*]
When will old man Hasler break down
And come up with that seven-and-a-half cent raise?

SINGING BOY I exits D.R. GIRL returns to group R.

SINGING BOY II [*Crosses U.R. to C., sings to* 2ND HELPER. *who has entered from D.L.*].
How in the hell can I buy me a swell new second-hand car
On that salary he pays?

SINGING GIRL I (POOPSIE)   What do you think of the new superintendent?

SINGING GIRL II [*Spoken*].   He's cute.

SINGING GIRL III [*Spoken*].   He'll never last.

SINGING GIRL IV [*Sings*].   He's kind of fresh for a new sup'rintendent.

BRENDA [*Spoken*].   I like a man with zip.

SINGING GIRL V [*Spoken*].   You like a man, period!

All GIRLS laugh. HINES enters from U.R., crosses D.C. to exit D.R.

HINES.   All right girls. Cut out the laughing. Cut out the laughing. Tempus fugit. Tempus fugit.

HINES exits D.R.

GIRLS [*Imitating him*].   Waste—waste—waste!!!

HINES [*Re-entering D.R.*].   Hurry up.

HINES exits D.R.   Warn sound.

GIRLS I [*Sing*].   Hurry up, hurry up, hurry up, hurry up,
Hurry up, hurry up, hurry up, hurry up,

GIRLS II.   Can't waste time—can't waste time—
Can't waste time—can't waste time.

MEN.   When you're racing with the clock
When you're racing with the clock
And the second hand doesn't understand
That your back may break and your fingers ache

ALL.   And your constitution isn't made of rock

GIRLS.   Hurry up, [*Etc.*] Can't waste time [*Etc.*]

MEN.   It's a losing race when you're racing with the,
Racing with the,
Racing with the clock.

ALL.   Can't waste time,
Racing racing racing racing racing
Racing racing racing racing racing
Racing racing racing racing racing
Racing with the clock!

After applause for number—Gong Go
The CROWD breaks up as they go to lunch ad libbing. GIRL I
crosses from R. to D.L., calls back to GIRL II.

SINGING GIRL I [*Speaks*].   Lunch!! Hey, Mary, you going to the cafeteria?

SINGING GIRL II.   I'll meet you there.

SINGING GIRL I.   Swell.

The GIRLS and BOYS exit L. and R. Some of the BOYS push the trolley off R. SID enters from U.L. with CHARLEY. followed by the TWO HELPERS. SID crosses to second D.S. machine CHARLEY stops at U.S. machines. The TWO HELPERS cross to stage D.R.C., the 2ND HELPER carries a tool box which he sets D.R.
Music finishes.

SID.   We can fix this while they're at lunch. No, no, it's number 9.

CHARLIE crosses down to L. *of* SID, *and hands him pliers.*

CHARLIE. **Here you are.**

SID. **Thanks.** [*Kneels at No. 9 machine.*]

1ST HELPER [*Kneeling at tool box* C.]. **This new super won't last—a Chicago guy.**

2ND HELPER. **He don't belong in this town.** [*Kneeling.*]

1ST HELPER. **The whole second floor was broke down and they couldn't find him . . . he was fixing a boiler . . . and then he yells at me. I don't stand for that. There's plenty of other places I can work. I don't have to take that off nobody.**

SID. **Give me a screw-driver.** [*Rising.*]

1ST HELPER [*Slowly gets tool and rises*]. **You know what they're paying at the packing plant? Ninety-three up. That ain't hay neither.**

MABEL enters from U.R.

SID. **Screw-driver!**

1ST HELPER *throws tool to* SID. MABEL *crosses to* R. *of* SID.

MABEL. **Oh, Mr. Sorokin.**

SID. **Yes, Mabel?**

MABEL. **Mr. Hasler's gone to the shipping room. He wants you right away.**

SID. **I've got to finish this. I can't . . .**

MABEL. **Yes, yes, I know . . . Mr. Hasler's kind of difficult sometimes.** [*Crosses to* L.C.] **You're the third superintendent we've had this year.**

SID. **And I'm the last one you'll have this year, Mabel, 'cause I want this job.**

1ST HELPER [*Sotto voce*]. **You don't say.**

MABEL. **Now you're talking, boy.**

SID [*To* 1ST HELPER]. **Bring me a switch.** [*Kneels down.*]

MABEL. **I'll tell him you're awful busy.**

MABEL exits D.L.

SID. **Thanks.**

1ST HELPER. **And let me tell you something else. They're paying eighty-four up at the casket company.**

SID [*Crossing down to* 1ST HELPER]. **My gosh, you'd be a sensation up at the casket company. Maybe you could get a job as a tester and just lie around in coffins all day long. Now hurry it up.**

1ST HELPER. **I'm hurrying.**

SID. **Well, hurry faster.**

SID *pushes him.* 1ST HELPER *sprawls on floor* D.R.

1ST HELPER. **Hey, you can't do that to me.**

SID [*Finding switch in tool box*]. **The hell I can't. I just did.** [*He crosses back up to* CHARLIE *and speaks to him.*] **Got the screws?** [*Kneels down.*]

1ST HELPER [*Rising*]. **Well, I'll fix you.** [*Crosses to* R. *of* SID.] **I'm getting the Grievance Committee.**

SID. **Go get them. It'll give you something to do.**

1ST HELPER. **I don't have to take that stuff off nobody.**

SID [*Rising from machine and facing him*]. **Go away . . . boy . . . you bother me.**

1ST HELPER [*Crossing to* D.L.]. **I'll show you . . . on my weak arm too.**

1ST HELPER *exits* D.L. Warn Cue 5.

CHARLIE. **That Grievance Committee can start quite a rhubarb.**

SID. **This whole town's a rhubarb.**

CHARLIE. **You'll get used to it.**

SID. **I hope so. We've got to have a larger switch and we'll need a fuse.**

CHARLIE [*Crossing* D.L.]. **I'll go down to the storehouse.** [*He exits* D.L.]

SID [*To* 2ND HELPER]. **Give him a hand.**

2ND HELPER *starts out* L. *slowly—(as he passes* SID

Move! ! !

Cue 5.

Music No. 3. " A NEW TOWN IS A BLUE TOWN "

2ND HELPER *rushes off* D.L.

SID [*Turns* U.S.—*slaps table. Crosses* R. *to window. Sings*].

A new town is a blue town. [*Looking out of window.*]
A "who do you know" and "show me what you can do" town.
There's no red carpet at your feet. [*Crosses* C.]
If you're not tough they'll try to beat you down [*Stopping* R.C.]
In a new blue town [*Sits in chair* C.]
The old town
It's not like the old town,
You don't take long to find that you're in a cold town.
But you know you can't lick it.
Didn't buy a round-trip ticket

To this
[*Rises—crosses* C.—*Hands in pockets, crosses* D.S.C
Cold, cold new blue town.
Well nobody asked me to come here
And nobody asked me to stay.
Made up my own mind
And I know that I'll find my own way
[*Crosses* L.C.—*hands out of pockets.*]
Since that first day
When I said " Hi town!"
[*Step* C.]
They've damned-well tried to make me say " Goodbye town"
But I won't leave until I make it my town.
They'll see. [*Puts screwdriver in box.*]
This one-horse, two-bit, hick-of-a-new town
Ain't gonna lick me.

Music continues under dialogue. HINES *enters from* D.L. *followed*
by HASLER *and* GLADYS.

HINES.   **Mr. Hasler's looking for you!** [*Crosses to behind the tool box.*]
HASLER.   **Did you get lost?**
SID.   **I had to fix the number 9 machine.**
HASLER.   **I expected you in the shipping room.**

HASLER *crosses to* U.S. *machines.* GLADYS *crosses to* SID *and pats*
his arm.

GLADYS.   **Don't pay any attention to him, Sid.**   [*Crosses* R.]
SID.   **Thanks.**

Warn Cue 6.

SID *crosses up to No. 9 machine.* GLADYS *crosses* R.   HINES *grabs*
her by the R. *arm as she passes him and spins her round. She is*
then R. *of him.*

HINES.   **When did you get so familiar with him . . . Sid, what does that**
   mean?
GLADYS.   **It doesn't mean anything. I just like to be friendly.**
HINES.   **Friendly? You're always flirting.**
GLADYS.   **Oooh ! ! !** [*She exits* D.R.]
HINES.   **Dancing on the green! Juke boxes!**

HINES *exits* D.R.

HASLER [*Turns to* SID]. **After this, when I send for you I'll expect you.** [*Starts*
to exit U.R.] **That's the way we run things around here.**

SID *steps* U.   HASLER *exits* U.R.

SID [*Sings. Crosses* D.C.]
Since that first day
When I said " Hi town "
They've damned well tried to make me say " Goodbye town "
But I won't leave until I make it my town,
They'll see
This one-horse, two-bit, hick-of-a new town
Ain't gonna LICK me.

Cue 6.

After number SID *turns* U.S., *kneels at machine.* CHARLIE *and*
MABEL *enter* D.L. CHARLIE *crosses to* R. *of* SID. MABEL *crosses*
to L. *of* SID.

MABEL.   **Mr. Sorokin! I told you to be careful. When I heard about your**
   beating up that boy . . .
SID.   **I didn't beat him up.**
MABEL.   **He's dangling his arm like it was hurt terrible.**
SID.   **Let him take it up with the committee.**

MABEL *crosses to* R.C.

CHARLIE.   **He's doing that, don't worry. Here comes Babe Williams.**
SID.   **I'll be delighted to talk to her.**

1ST HELPER *enters from* D.R., *followed by* BABE, BRENDA *and* MAE.
2ND HELPER *follows them on. They all cross to* D.L.

1ST HELPER.   **All right, Mister. Here's the Grievance Committee.**
SID [*Turns and sees that the committee consists of* BABE]. **Oh, is this the Committee?**
   [*Crossing down to* R. *of* BABE.]
BABE.   **That's right, Mr. Sorokin. This is the Committee.**
SID [*Turning to* CHARLIE]. **Charlie, this Grievance Committee IS different**
BABE.   **Never mind the snow job.**
SID.   **I'm sorry.** [*Steps in.*] **All right . . . Look, I shoved the kid. What's**
   the next move?

BABE. **He says you hit him.**
SID. **No, I just . . .** [*Starts to illustrate but stops short.*] **Look, Miss Wilson . . . I've got quite a few problems on my hands right now.**
MAE. **Her name is Miss Williams.**
BABE. **What's the difference?**
SID. **Oh, I'm sorry. Miss Williams.**
BABE. **It doesn't matter.**
MAE. **Well, he ought to know the Committee's right name.**
BABE. **Take it easy. Look Mr. Sorokin. I have quite a few problems of my own right now. This helper says you socked him.**
SID. **He does?**
1ST HELPER. **Yes, I do.**
SID. **Let's say I shoved him. It sounds more refined.**
HINES enters U.R., crosses to C.
HINES. **Mr. Sorokin, Mr. Hasler wants to see you in his office right away.**
SID [*Turns to him*]. **Tell him to . . . Tell him okay.**
HINES. **This is a crisis. The tops are fifteen minutes behind the bottoms.**
HINES crosses R. to MABEL.
SID. **Let's be practical. This is a lot of damned nonsense.**
Warn sound.
BABE. **We don't happen to think so, Mr. Sorokin. You're not supposed to strike an employee. We have rules about that.**
SID. **I know. For both sides I hope. Listen, Miss Williams, I'll spread it on the table. This young man needs vocational guidance.**
BABE. **You think so?**
SID. **He wants to be a Bank President. I don't believe he's happy as a factory helper.**
MAE. **I don't see what all this has to do with it.**
BABE [*To* MAE]. **Forget it.** [*To* 1ST HELPER.] **It seems you haven't made a very good impression on our new superintendent.**
1ST HELPER. **He ain't got no right to push me around. Especially on my weak arm.**
Gong go.
The WORKERS begin entering R. and L.
Warn Cue 8 and 9, Flys, Sound.
SID. **Look, Miss Williams. I've got to get this factory going. Can't we take this up later?**
BABE. **Of course we can, Mr. Sorokin. That's in the rule book too.** [*Crossing* C.—*pushes* 1ST HELPER R. *To* 1ST HELPER.) **Go tell the nurse to check your arm . . . then send me a report.**
2ND HELPER picks up tool box—carries it off D.L.
1ST HELPER [*Crosses to* R.]. **Can't shove me around. It was broke once already.**
Exits D.R.
SID [*Stepping* D.S., *stopping* BABE, *who is* R. *of him*]. **Thanks for your co-operation, Miss Williams.**
BABE. **It's all in the rule book.**
SID. **I must read that rule book sometime.**
BABE. **You certainly should.**
BABE crosses to L. as if to go—SID'S next speech stops her.
SID. **All I have to say is that you're the cutest Grievance Committee I ever had to deal with.**
Gong go.
SID exits U.R., followed by MABEL. BABE exits D.L. The GIRLS resume their work.

Music No. 4.   " RACING WITH THE CLOCK "   (Reprise)

HINES [*Speaks. Crosses* U.C.]. **All right, girls. Hurry up. I've got my stop watch on you.**
GIRLS [*Singing*].   When you're racing with the clock
                     When you're racing with the clock
                     And the second hand doesn't understand
HINES starts beating time with his foot, as the music gets faster and faster.
                     That your back may break and your fingers ache
                     And your constitution isn't made of rock.
                     [*Repeat.*]
                     It's a losing race when you're racing with the,
                     Racing with the,
                     Racing with the Clock.
[*Last four lines, repeat ad lib.. (accel.) with alternate groups vocally.*]
On 1st " losing RACE "—Cue 8.,.Elevator Cloth in.
When Elevator Cloth is in—Cue 9

ACT I—SCENE 3. THE HALLWAY

This is a hallway in the factory. On the wall are various notices.
In the stage L. panel is an elevator door.
As the lights come up on the scene, PREZ *and* JOE *enter from* D.L.

PREZ. [*Crossing to* C.]. You elected me president, you've got to have confidence in me.

JOE [*At* L.C.]. Sure, but I only said . . .

PREZ. Look, this is no time to be talking about no ultimatums and no strikes.

JOE. Yes, but that seven-and-a-half cents . . .

PREZ. Wait a minute . . . there ain't no question but we're going to get that seven-and-a-half cents raise. Other companies are paying it and we're entitled to it, but we got to be smart. Wait till old Hasler's got so many orders in, he can't afford to shut the factory down. Then we got him.

JOE. You bet.

PREZ. You bet.

> PREZ *taps* JOE *playfully*—JOE *exits* D.L. MAE, POOPSIE, BABE,
> BRENDA *and* GIRLS *enter* D.R. *and cross to* C.

MAE. Well.

POOPSIE. Hiya, Prez.

PREZ. Hi.

MAE. I wouldn't want no super to try and shove me around.

PREZ [*Crossing to* BABE]. Say Babe, what about that kid that got hit. What'd the super have to say for himself?

BABE. That's one for the birds, Prez. That kid hasn't even got a bruise on his arm. He's a faker.

PREZ. You think so, huh, Babe?

BABE. Sure he's a phoney. If that guy Sorokin ever really hit him he'd break him in two.

PREZ. Okay.

> PREZ *crosses below* BABE *and exits* D.R.

POOPSIE. Mr. Sorokin is so-o-o-o strong . . .

GIRL I. He's so wonderful.

BABE [*Looking from one to the other*]. What's this?

POOPSIE [*Steps to* BABE R.C.]. The new super, I think he's simply woo-woo, don't you?

BABE. I didn't notice.

POOPSIE. I noticed.

GIRL II. I thought Babe was noticin' too.

BRENDA. Yeah . . . she lit up.

BABE. You girls are getting . . .

BRENDA. Love comes at last to Babe Williams. [*Taps* BABE *playfully on head.*]

BABE [*Crossing* R.]. Oh, get off it! I hardly looked at the guy. I'm the Grievance Committee. LOVE!—are you nuts?

> *From far* R.—*She crosses from* C. *to* D.R.

Music No. 5. " I'M NOT AT ALL IN LOVE "

POOPSIE. Some people can't tell when it hits them . . .

> GIRLS *gossip in groups.* Warn Cue 10.

BABE. Bah! [*From far* R., *in front of truck. Sings.*]
> All you gotta do is say "hello" to a man
> And they have you whispering in his ear.
> All you gotta do is be polite with him,
> And they have you spending the night with him.
> If there's a guy you merely have a beer with
> > GIRLS *turn to listen to* BABE.
> They've got you setting the wedding date.
> It seems they've just got to have some DIRT
> > to bend your ear with
> So before they start I herewith state [*Leans on truck*]
> I'm not at all in love, not at all in love, not I.
> Not a bit, not a mite, [*Sits on truck* R.C.]
> Tho' I'll admit he's quite a hunk of guy,
> But he's not my cup of tea,
> Not my cup of tea, not he,
> Not an ounce, not a pinch,
> He's just an inch too sure of himself for ME.
> > Cue 10.

[BABE *turns back on girls, puts feet up on truck.*]

BRENDA [*From* C.].
> Well of course you've noticed that manly physique and that
> look in his eye.

11

Say I'm sure he can cut most any man down to size.
SINGING GIRL I [*From* L.C.].
He must be as fierce as a tiger when he's mad
POOPSIE [*Crosses to* L. *of* BABE, *and crouches*].
And I'll bet he cries like a little boy when he's sad.
BABE [*Crosses to* D.L.].
But I'm not at all in love, not at all in love, not I.
Not a straw, not a hair,
I don't care [*Back to* C.] if he's as strong as a lion
Or if he has the rest of you sighin'
You may be sold [*Crosses back to* R.C.] but this girl ain't buyin',
[*Crosses to truck—sits on it.* GIRLS *wheel her toward* C.]
I'm not at all in love.
GIRLS [*Wheeling her towards* C.]
She's not at all in love, not at all in love, oh no!
BABE.   Not a pin, not a crumb.
GIRLS.   Must be summer heat that gives her that glow,
[*Wheeling her* L.C.]
'Cause she's not at all in love, not at all in love she cries.
BABE.   Not a snip, not a bite.
GIRLS.   Must be the light from the ceiling shining there in her eyes.
GIRL *mimics debonair man with moustache.*
He's young and handsome and smart and we can't get over it.
GIRL *jabs* MAE *playfully—*MAE *squeals and fakes swoon.*
BABE.   But this lady's heart he doesn't affect a bit.
GIRLS [*Wheeling her far* R.].
It's easy to see that her daffy grin is the grin she always wears.
And she's breathless because she ran up a flight of stairs.
[*They push* BABE *on truck across to* L.]
GIRL I [*Spoken*].   Obviously!
3 GIRLS [*Spoken*].   Naturally!
ALL GIRLS [*Spoken*].   Certainly!

BABE *is thrown off truck into* SID'S *arms—he has just come out of
the elevator.* CHARLIE *enters with him and exits* D.L.

SID [*Spoken*].   Excuse me.
BABE [*Taking bite of apple. Spoken*].   Excuse me.
SID [*Spoken*].   I'm sorry.

SID *crosses from* L. *to* R. *past the line of* GIRLS *and exits* D.R. *The*
GIRLS *gaze after him until he is off, then stare back at* BABE.
GIRL *pushes truck across from* R. *to* L.
Warn Cue 11 and 12, Flys, Sound (Scene 4)

GIRL I [*Spoken*].   Obviously!
GIRL II [*Spoken*].   Naturally!
GIRL III [*Spoken*].   Certainly!
ALL.   Ha!
[*Sung.*]   She's not at all in love, not at all in love, not she.
BABE.   No, I'm not.
GIRLS.   Not a dot.
BABE.   Not a touch.
GIRLS.   No not much.
BABE   When I fall in love there'll be no doubt about it,
'Cause you will know from the way that I shout it.
GIRLS [*Spoken quietly. Lean forward—hands on knees*].   You're shouting!
BABE [*Whispers*].   I haven't fallen.
GIRLS [*Whisper*].   She hasn't fallen.
BABE [*Stamps foot*].
I'm not at all in love.
GIRLS.   She's not at all in love.

ALL *hold the picture for applause.* BABE *breaks it by making a face
at the* GIRLS. *At the same time the Orchestra pick up the reprise
Some* GIRLS *wheel* BABE *on truck off* D.L. *Others exit* D.R.

Music No. 6.   "I'M NOT AT ALL IN LOVE"   *Change*

On Music reprise—Cue 11.
When lights out—Elevator Cloth away.
When Cloth away and office desk set—Cue 12.

ACT I—SCENE 4. THE OFFICE

This is SOROKIN'S *office, where he has a desk set* R.C. *Behind this desk there is a swivel armchair. At the* L. *side of the desk is an upright chair. On the desk are numerous papers, letter tray, blotter, ink-stand, etc. At the* L. *end of the desk is a modern telephone, and at the* R. *end of the desk is a dictaphone.* U.S. *of the desk and slightly* R. *is a doorway. The back wall has two windows, each equipped with adjustable blinds.* U.S.L. *is another doorway.* D.S. *of this doorway is* MABEL'S *desk which is enormous and is littered with ledgers, files, trays, letters, etc.* D.S. *of this desk is a large filing cabinet. On the desk is an old-fashioned typewriter and an upright telephone.*

As the lights come up MABEL *is seated at her desk typing.* GLADYS *enters* L. *carrying a big ledger.*

GLADYS [*Crosses to desk* R.]. **Got those figures for Mr. Hasler?**

MABEL [*Still typing*]. **They're in the file.**

GLADYS. **Where's your boss?**

MABEL. **On the first floor. A couple of the girls had a fight.**

Phone rings.

MABEL *answers the phone.* GLADYS *sees there is no further conversation and exits* L.

Superintendent's office—yes, Sid—Dolores Paradise, that's her name. She's supposed to be very elegant. She can sew a button on a fly like she was pouring tea at the White House. [*Knock on door.*] **Come!**

POOPSIE *enters* R., *crosses to* L.C.

Oh yes, she can pull hair all right! [*Hangs up. Turns to* POOPSIE.] **Them girls spoiled a piece of goods. When Mr. Hasler finds that out, there'll be blood all over the place.**

POOPSIE. **Wanta buy a ticket for the picnic?**

MABEL [*Gets purse from desk drawer*]. **Might as well get it over with.**

POOPSIE. **One dollar. And all the beer you can guzzle.**

MABEL [*Searching through purse for dollar*]. **No beer for me. It gives me the heartburn something awful.**

HINES *enters* R.

HINES. **Me too.**

MABEL. **You!**

HINES *crosses* L. *below them and stands* D.L.

POOPSIE. **You gonna do your knife-throwing act this year, Mr. Hines?**

HINES. **I suppose so.**

GLADYS *enters* L., *carrying ledger, crosses to desk* R., *and puts ledger on* L. *end of it.*

There always seems to be a demand for it. [*Leans against files.*]

POOPSIE. **Was you honest on the real stage?**

GLADYS. **That's where I first met him, Poopsie. He was throwing knives at a woman at the Majestic Theatre.** [*Starts to write note at desk.*]

POOPSIE. **Is Mr. Hasler in his office?**

GLADYS. **No.**

MABEL [*Handing money*]. **Here. One hard-earned dollar, and I hope the ham ain't as salty as it was at the last union picnic. I was dried up for a week after.**

POOPSIE. **Thanks.**

Exits U.R., *leaving the door off the latch.* GLADYS *has put the note on Sid's desk.* HINES *watches it suspiciously. He becomes tense.*

HINES [*Crossing to* L. *of* GLADYS]. **Hey, what're you doing? Leaving him a note? Huh?**

GLADYS *gives him a dirty look.*

Carrying on with Sorokin, huh?

GLADYS. **Oh, Vernon.**

HINES. **I saw you leave that note on his desk. I'm not blind. That's why you wore that low neck dress to work today.**

GLADYS [*She has on a very modest dress*]. **You make me scream, Vernon—you just make me scream.**

HINES. **All right then, what's in it? I dare you tell me what's in it.**

GLADYS [*Hands him note*]. **Read it, then go and cut your throat.**

HINES [*Grabs note, steps* D.S. *and reads*]. **Okay payroll seven thousand five hundred and two dollars and one cent.**

GLADYS. **That means I love you in the Morse Code.**

MABEL. **Ain't you ashamed of yourself, Hineszie?**

HINES *hangs his head.*

GLADYS [*Crosses* L.]. **Now that we got that all settled, do you think you could trust me as far as the ladies' room?**

Exits U.L.   Warn Cue 13.

HINES [*Sits on chair* L. *of desk*].   **I'll never be jealous again, Mabel—never.**
GLADYS [*Comes back suddenly*].   **Maybe I'll give you cause someday.**
                                          Exits.
MABEL [*Rising and turning her chair to face front. Crosses to* U.L.C. *to window—looks out*].   **Oh, Hineszie, Hineszie!**

                    Music No. 7.   **" I'LL NEVER BE JEALOUS AGAIN "**

HINES [*Spoken. Leaning on desk*].   **I learned my lesson. I'll never be jealous again.**
MABEL [*Spoken. Turns from window to face* HINES].   **You stick to it now.**
HINES [*Spoken*].   **Absolutely**
MABEL [*Sings. Points to* HINES—*crosses* D. *to* R. *of him*].
      THAT'S **easier said than done.**
                                                          Cue 13.
HINES.   **I can do it.**
MABEL.   **I knew it, but let's take an example just for fun.** [*Crosses to above desk.*]
         Picture this, you're sitting and waiting for her to come back from a date.
HINES.   **There I am, I'm sitting and waiting for her to come back from a date.**
MABEL [*Points front with* L. *hand*].
         Here she comes, her blouse is unbuttoned, her stockings are not very straight.
HINES.   **Here she comes, her blouse is unbuttoned, her stockings are not very straight.**
MABEL.   **Later on she gets a bouquet with a card in it saying " To baby, you were great ".**
      [*Leans towards him. Spoken.*]
         Well, Hineszie, what would you do then?
HINES [*Rising*].
         I would trust her, I would trust her,
         By George I swear I would trust her,
         No, I'll never be jealous again [*Sits firmly.*]
MABEL [*Speaks—steps to* L. *of him—leans over his shoulder, motions ahead*].   **Nice work Hineszie. Let's take another example.**
[*Sings.*] **Picture this, you've nothing to do so you drop in to chat for a while.**
HINES.   **There I am with nothing to do so I drop in to chat for a while.**
MABEL.   **Something's up, the window is open and Gladys is forcing a smile.**
HINES.   **Something's up, the window is open and Gladys is forcing a smile.**
MABEL.   **Then you see a shirt and a tie and a pair of pants in a nice, neat, little pile.**
[*Speaks.*] **Well, Hineszie?**
HINES [*Rises*]
         I would trust her, I would trust her,
         By George, I swear I would trust her,
         No, I'll never be jealous
         I'll never never never never never never never never never be
         Jealous again!
MABEL [*Speaks*].   **That's the stuff, Hineszie. You're practically cured!**
HINES [*Puts hands on her shoulders*].
         There will be no more nightmares to sleep through,
         No more keyholes to peep through,
         No more bushes to creep through!
                                                      Warn Cue 13a.
MABEL [*Stepping* L,]
         That's some plan,
         Well now that you're a new man,
                              HINES *steps to* MABEL.
         Picture this, you go to your sweetie's apartment, you borrowed the keys!
HINES.   **There I am, I go to my sweetie's apartment, I borrowed the keys.**
MABEL.   **There she is, she's giving a sailor a very affectionate squeeze.**
HINES.   **There she is, she's giving a sailor a very affectionate squeeze:**
MABEL.   **Then, to boot, she tells you she was in the arms of her Cousin who's back from overseas.**
HINES [*Speaks*].   **Her cousin from overseas? Do you expect me to believe that?**
MABEL [*Speaks. Steps away—looks at him sternly—arms crossed*].   **Hineszie!**
HINES [*Sings*].
         I would trust her, I would trust her,
         By George, I swear, I would trust her.

No, I'll never be jealous,
I'll never never never never never never never never never never,
Never never never never never never,
Never be jealous again.

Cue 13a.
Warn Cue 14.
They go into soft snoe dance. In the middle of dance Warn Cue 14
*During the end section of the dance he whirls her and seats her on
her chair.* Cue 14.
When she is seated he backs R. *and exits* U.R.
HASLER *and* SID *enter* U.R. SID *crosses to his desk, looks at paper*
HASLER *walks up and down in anger until applause fades.*

HASLER [*Crossing to* MABEL *at desk* L., *and clapping his hands*]. **What right has the
Union to run their coca-cola machine with our electricity?** [*Stepping* C.]
It's just as Walter Winchell said last night. [*Breaks off suddenly, turns
to* SID.] **Do you listen to Walter Winchell, Sorokin?**

SID. **Well, I'm rather flexible in the matter.**

HASLER [*Crosses to* SID R.C., *back of desk*]. **Say, he has got their number—keen
mind—one of the greatest thinkers in the country today. Should listen
to him every night. It ought to be in every executive's contract.** [*He sees
ledger on desk.*] **What's this? This book shouldn't be left lying around.**
[*Picks up ledger.*]

GLADYS *enters* L., *patting her hair.* HASLER *screams.*

Gladys!

GLADYS [*Stopping petrified in doorway*]. **Yes?**

HASLER. **Where have you been?**

GLADYS [*Almost weeping*]. **I been to the ladies' room. Isn't that all right?**

HASLER. **But this book—**

GLADYS [*Hand at throat—relieved*]. **Oh, Mr. Hasler, you scared the life out of me.
Look.** [*Clutching key.*] **I've got the key around my neck. It's all right.**

HASLER [*Pounding out his words*]. **I don't want it left lying around. Is that
clear?** [*Hands book to* GLADYS.]

GLADYS. **Yes, Mr. Hasler.** [*She takes the book in a flushed humiliation and exits.*]

HASLER [*Standing* C.]. **If I can't trust Gladys, who can I trust?**

SID [*Steadily*]. **I wouldn't know.**

HASLER [*Pause—sudden realisation*]. **What was my book doing here, anyhow?**

*Siezed with a sudden desire to find out, he bolts from the room,
following* GLADYS. SID *and* MABEL *look at each other.*

MABEL [*At desk*]. **Say, Sid, who is this Walter Winchell he's always talking
about?**

SID. **He plays third base for the New York Yankees.** [*Sits desk* R.] **The old
man's got a bad case of bookitis, hasn't he?**

MABEL. **Oh, yes.**

SID [*Opening desk drawer—looks for something inside*]. **I wonder if he's got a
skeleton locked in there. Say, Mabel . . . tell me something. What
kind of a girl is this Babe Williams?**

MABEL [*Turns in chair to face* SID]. **Babe? She's peppy.**

SID [*Working on papers*]. **Is she married?**

MABEL [*Leaning on chair*]. **No, not quite.**

SID. **What do you mean, not quite?**

MABEL. **Well, she was close once. She was engaged to the Johnson boy.
Then one time at a football game she pushed him off the end of the grand-
stand and gave him a concussion. That broke the engagement.**

HASLER *enters from* L. *Crosses to* C.

SID. **Outdoor girl.**

HASLER [*Crosses* C.]. **Gladys is crying. She's hysterical.** [*He imitates her sobs.*
To MABEL.] **Gump . . .** [*To* SID.] **Gump . . .**

MABEL. **She brought the ledger up here to enter the cost totals, Mr. Hasler.**

HASLER. **Well, why in hell couldn't somebody say so. My gosh!**

Exits U.L. Warn sound.

SID [*In phone*]. **Give me ladies' pants. Is this you, Prez? Sorokin speaking.
Say,** [*Leaning back.*] **whatever happened to that complaint from the
Helper I'm supposed to have socked . . . I'd like to get it settled. Would
you send the Grievance Committee up to my office—**[MABEL *turns to* SID.]
—no, right away, thanks. [*Hangs up.*]

MABEL. **I heard you had an eye for her.**

SID. **You hear things easy around this place.** [*Sharp look at her.*] **First thing
you know they'll be talking about us.**

MABEL. **Oh, don't think it hasn't been mentioned.** [*Turns back to her work.*]

SID [*Picking up mouthpiece and flipping key on dictaphone*]. **Memo, cutting foreman. Too many rejects.**

On rayon crepe numbers.

Phone rings.

Come in.

Knock on door.

BABE enters R.

MABEL. **Hello!**

SID [*To* BABE]. **Have a seat.**

BABE. **Thank you.**

BABE crosses to chair L. of desk, glances at SID, decides it is too near him, then moves chair to C. and sits.

SID. **Look into it and report back.** [*Replaces mouthpiece.*]

MABEL [*On phone*]. **Yes, Mr. Hasler! I will be right there.** [*Hangs up,—Pause.*] **Gladys is still crying and he wants me to take a couple of letters.**

Crosses to door L.—looks back wisely at BABE and SID. Exits U.L.

SID. **I wanted to talk to you about that assault and battery case.**

BABE. **Oh! Well, we thought we would just forget about that, Mr. Sorokin.**

SID. **Yes?**

BABE. **Yeah. We all know that injured arm was a lot of nonsense. To tell you the truth we've had trouble with him before.**

SID. **I can believe that. If you only knew what I had to go through to get him to kick across with a screwdriver—I'd have been justified if I HAD socked him.**

BABE. **Well, we won't go into that. But anyhow we have it down in our books as a slight nudge.** [*Pause, looks front, then rises quickly and steps L. and U.S. of chair.*]

SID [*Rising quickly, stopping her*]. **Personally, I think a little physical punishment is good for people once in a while.**

BABE. **Oh, do you, Captain Bligh?**

SID. **No—not exactly. Sit down for a second will you, Miss Williams. I want to talk to you.**

BABE sits and so does he.

How about a date?

BABE. **What?**

Warn Cue 15, Sound.

SID. **How about going out to dinner some night?**

BABE. **Well, I don't know.**

SID. **Maybe check up on some of the local hot spots?**

BABE. **Thanks. But I don't think so.** [*She rises—crosses to back of chair and leans on it.*]

SID [*Turns front*]. **What is this strange power I have over women?**

BABE. **It really wouldn't work, not at all.**

SID. **Looks like I struck out that time.**

BABE. **Its nothing personal.**

SID rises—steps to her intimately.

But you see you're the Superintendent and I'm the Grievance Committee.

Music No. 8. **INTRODUCTION TO "HEY THERE"**

BABE crosses—exits R. SID looks after her. After her exit SID sits at desk, flips on dictaphone and picks up mouthpiece.

SID [*Speaks*]. **Memo: Time-Keeper. Be sure all girls fill out time cards properly and — —** [*Shuts it off and then back on again.*] **Memo to Sid Sorokin.**

Music No. 8A. **"HEY THERE"**

SID [*Sings into dictaphone*].

HEY THERE!

Cue 15.

**You with the stars in your eyes,
Love never made a fool of you,
You used to be too wise!
Hey there! You on that high flying cloud.
Though she won't throw a crumb to you,
You think some day she'll come to you;
Better forget her,**

[*Looks off R. at door.*] **Her with her nose in the air,
She has you dancing on a string,
Break it and she won't care!
Won't you take this advice I hand you like a brother?
Or are you not seeing things too clear,**

> Are you just too far gone to hear,
> Is it all going in one ear
> And out the other?

He replaces the mouthpiece.   Sound Go.
The machine has been left on and he hears the sound of his own voice coming back.

MACHINE.   **Hey there! You with the stars in your eyes,**
SID [*Looking at machine. Spoken*].   **Who, me?**
MACHINE.   **Love never made a fool of you,**
SID [*Sitting back*].   **Not until now!**
MACHINE.   **You used to be too wise!**
SID [*Rises—crosses to* U.R. *to window*].   **Yeah, I was once.**
MACHINE.   **Hey there,**
SID [*Looking back—then looking out window*].   **I hear you.**
MACHINE.   **You on that high flying cloud,**

SID *turns to machine.*

> **Though she won't throw a crumb to you,**

SID.   **Don't rub it in.**

Warn Cues 16 and 17, Flys.

MACHINE.   **You think some day she'll come to you;**
SID [*Crosses to desk, picks up paper*].   **Aw, shut up!**
MACHINE.   **Better forget her,**
SID [*Throws paper down. Sings*].

> **Forget her.**

SID *crosses to chair* C.

MACHINE.   **Her with her nose in the air.**
SID.   **Her with her nose in the air.** [*Crosses to* L. *of desk.*]
MACHINE.   **She has you dancing on a string,**
SID.   **A puppet on a string.**
MACHINE.   **Break it and she won't care.**
SID [*Leaning on a chair*].

> **She won't care for me.** [*Crosses back to desk.*]

MACHINE.   **Will you**
BOTH.   **Take this advice I hand you like a brother.**
SID [*Flips off machine*].

> **Or am I not seeing things too clear?** [*Flips machine on.*]

MACHINE.   **Are you too much in love to hear?**
SID [*Sits at desk. Flips machine off*].

> **Is it all going in one ear and out the other?**

On cue: " —and out THE other."—Cue 16, Black drop and Picnic, Gauze in.
When Gauze in—Cue 17.

SCENE 5. PICNIC CROSSOVER

The lights come up revealing a wooded path. People are crossing from L. *to* R., *going to a picnic. They are carrying beach balls, rubber animals, baskets of food, etc. A group of 6* BOYS *enter first, and cross to* R.

1ST HELPER [*Stops* C. *stage, in baseball uniform with back to audience so they can see the Sleep Tite sign on his back, shouts to* BOYS *running off* R.].   **Hey, wait a minute.**
[*To* BOY *off* L.] **Hey, Eddie.**

Another BOY *joins them and exits* D.R. POOPSIE, *in bathing suit, crosses from* L. *to* R. *The* SALESMAN, *enters from* D.L. *with* BRENDA.

SALESMAN.   **I love these picnics . . . I always come back from the road for them. Say, on this last trip I sold a lot of Sleep Tite pajamas. Believe me.**

2 DANCING GIRLS *follow* SALESMAN *and* BRENDA.

BRENDA.   **You did, eh?**
SALESMAN.   **I knocked them for a loop in Massillon, Chillicothe, Van Wert, Napoleon. Finest season I ever had.**

SALESMAN *and* BRENDA *exit* D.R.
MAE *enters from* D.L. *with a* GIRL, *followed by two more* GIRLS. *They all cross from* L. *to* R.

MAE.   **Well, I'll have to make an announcement about the mix-up.** [*Stops* L.C., *then turns and continues across* R.] **It seems there ain't going to be enough baked beans to go around**
A GIRL.   **Oh, Mae.**
MAE.   **But there's plenty of potato salad . . . So them that doesn't care for beans can go heavily on the potato salad and vice versa.**

The GIRLS *exit* D.R. CHARLIE *and* JOE *carry a beer keg from* L. *to* R. GIRL *follows with spigot.* PREZ *enters from* D.L., *followed by* GLADYS. PREZ *is carrying a suitcase.*

PREZ [*Crossing to* C.].   **Where's Hineszie, Gladys?**

GLADYS *enters* L. *crosses to him.*

GLADYS.   **He couldn't keep up with me.**

PREZ [*Puts case down* C.].   **Boy, they gotta be good to keep up with you, and this is the day I say . . . Let yourself go, huh?**

GLADYS.   **You want to go someplace?**

PREZ.   **Aw, you know what I mean.** [*Turns away . . . upends suitcase.*] **Say, that's a mighty nifty outfit you got on.** [*Sits on suitcase.*] **I go for that.**

GLADYS.   **I don't know. I brought a dress along too. Hineszie says this outfit's too revealing.**

PREZ [*Rises*].   **It ain't too nothing. You tell Hineszie to go roll a hoop down Main Street.**

GLADYS *crosses below* PREZ *to* R.C.

You have class, honey. You're beautiful. [*He puts his arms around her.*]

GLADYS.   **I know I'm beautiful. Probably the most beautiful girl north of Keokuk, Iowa. But you got a wife, Prez.** [*Pushes his hands away. Turns to* PREZ.]

PREZ.   **Aw forget that. Her and me is total strangers. Listen Baby . . .**

Music No. 9.   "HER IS"   (*Verse*)

[*Sings.*] **I wouldn't never tell this to nobody else but you,**
          To nobody else but you I wouldn't never tell this,
          What I mean to say is, you're different from the rest,
          Baby, you're the best.

GLADYS *turns away from him.*

          And I wouldn't never tell this
          To nobody else. [*Puts arms around her.*]
          But you!

GLADYS [*Spoken*].   **Aw go on!** [*Throws his hands off.*] [*Sings.*] **Ha ha ha!**

PREZ [*Sings*].   **Ha ha ha!** [*Puts his arms around her.*]

GLADYS.   **Ha ha ha!** [*Puts his hands away—positively.*]

PREZ.   **Ha ha ha!**

GLADYS *pushes his hands off angrily.*

Music No. 9A.   "HER IS"   Chorus

PREZ.   **Her is a kinda doll what drives a fellow bats, isn't her?**

GLADYS.   **Her is** [*Turns away* R.—*back to him.*]

PREZ.   **Her has a kinda shape what really is the cats, hasn't her?** [*Puts his hands around her.*]

GLADYS.   **Her has!** [*Throws his hands off. Crosses to* L.]

PREZ [*Crosses to* R. *of her—Crossing* L.C.].
          My wife, she ain't understandin',
          She ain't like her is!
          This here ain't no line I'm handin'
          Or I should drop dead right where I'm standin'

GLADYS *crosses to* R. *below* PREZ—*he puts hands on her hips.*

          Her is a snappy dresser what is dressed to kill, isn't her?

GLADYS.   **Her is!**

PREZ [*Stepping far* R.—*hands on her hips*].
          Her is the only doll from which I get a thrill, isn't her?

GLADYS.   **Her is!** [*Crosses to* L. *of him—he takes her hand—she pulls other away.*]

PREZ.   **Her is runnin' away but her sure can bet**
          Him is gonna get her yet [*Pulls her to him hand-over-hand by her* R. *arm.*]
          I'm gonna get her yet!
        Pulls her around—embraces her—bending way over her.]

Music No. 9B.   "HER IS"   (*Dance*)

GLADYS [*Sings*].   **Ha ha ha!** [*Crosses to* R. *below* PREZ.]

PREZ.   **Ha ha ha!**

Dance—then repeat. GLADYS *gets kerchief back from* PREZ.
Warn Cues 18 and 19, Limes and Flys.
GLADYS *swings kerchief from side to side across rear.*

PREZ [*Rises, sings*].
          Her is a snappy dresser what is dressed to kill, isn't her?

GLADYS.   **Her is!**

PREZ.   **Her is the only doll from which I get a thrill, isn't her?**

GLADYS.   **Her is!**

PREZ.   Her is runnin' [*Picks up case.*] **away but her sure can bet**
         Him is gonna get her yet,   [*Stepping off* R.]

                              GLADYS *nods " yes " to him.*

         I'm gonna get her yet.

                              GLADYS *shakes her head " no " to audience.*
                              End of number on exit.
                              When GLADYS *at portal*—Cue 18, Lime out.
                              When lights out—Black drop away.
                              On start of " Sleep Tite " music—Cue 19.
                              On start of " Sleep Tite " vocal—Picnic Gauze away.

ACT I—SCENE 6.   THE PICNIC

                         As the lights come on we discover the FACTORY EMPLOYEES *at their
                         annual picnic. The scene is a wooded clearing.* R.C. *is a large
                         wooden target board with the silhouette of a woman painted on it.
                         Beside this is a small table with Hines' throwing knives on it.*
                         U.S.R. *is a long trestle table with a bench* D.S. *of it, and some stools*
                         U.S. *of it. On the table are beer bottles and cans, mugs and cartons.*
                         D.S.L. *is another long trestle table with a bench* U.S. *of it, and some
                         stools* D.S. *of it. On the table are more beer bottles and cans, mugs
                         and cartons, and a large beer barrel. The* EMPLOYEES *are grouped
                         on and around the tables and seats singing the company song.*
                         BABE *is standing on table* D.L.

                    Music No. 9C. **" SLEEP TITE "**

FACTORY EMPLOYEES [*Singing with actions*].

                    Sleep Tite,
                    Sleep Tite, Sleep Tite, we pledge our hearts
                    Devotion to thee, to thee.
                    Oh, Sleep Tite, Sleep Tite
                    Best in the land
                    With your reinforced buttons
                    And stretchproof waistband.

                              CROWD *applauds, and takes up new positions, sitting about the
                              stage.*

PREZ [*Stepping up on table, and helping* BABE *down, who sits on* R. *end of bench*].   **An'**
     now we're going to hear from another speaker. And at this time it gives
     me great pleasure to introduce to you at this time somebody and he
     don't actually need no introduction on account of we all know him and
     it's always a pleasure to have him with our midst and it gives me great
     pleasure to introduce to you our boss, Mr. Myron Hasler. Okay, Mr.
     Hasler.

                              Clapping and whistling—HASLER *rises.* PREZ *gets off table*—
                              HASLER *takes his place.*

HASLER [*Motioning with hands*].   **Thank you. I'm proud to be with you. We're**
     all members of a great industry. To that industry we owe our lives and
     our daily bread. In return, we must recognise the stern obligations
     placed upon us in these terrible times of economic upheaval and govern-
     mental chaos. I can never remember a time when competition was so
     ruthless, dealers so cantankerous, costs outrageous, and profit margins
     sunk so low. [*Points low.*] My good friends, pajamas are at the cross-
     roads; whether we go on to greater triumphs lies in you ; whether your
     company can weather the storm of rising costs is a grave question. I
     thank you.

                              Scattered applause. HASLER *off table and sits.*

PREZ [*Gets on table*].   **Thanks, Mr. Hasler. I'm sure we all enjoyed hearing**
     from you. And certainly nice to have you with us. Now, first thing after
     we leave the festive board there will be a knife-throwing exhibition by
     Professor Vernon Hines.

                              CROWD *laughs and cheers.*

HINES [*Rises and bows—he is on bench of table* R.].   **And I never miss.** [*He drinks
     and lurches, and is steadied by one of the girls*—CROWD *laughs.*]

PREZ.   **The baseball game will start at 1.30 sharp between the finishing room**
     and ladies' pants. This is a grudge contest and it ought to be good. Who
     wants to be my partner in the three-legged race? That's all [*He jumps
     off table.*]

                              CROWD *breaks up—ad libbing.*

DANCING GIRL I.   **Me for the baseball.** [*Rises—exits* D.R.]

DANCING GIRL II.   **I want to be in the three-legged race.**

POOPSIE [*Ringing bell*].   **Hear ye, hear ye, this way for the knife-throwing.**
                              Exits D.R.
PREZ. [*To* BRENDA].   **Hello, Gorgeous. How about another beer?**
BRENDA.   **All right.**
PREZ.   **This way.**
BRENDA.   **But the refreshment stand is . . .**
PREZ.   **No, no, it's out this way.** [*Takes her out* L.]
                              POOPSIE *enters from* D.R., *crosses* U.S.C., *exits* U.R.
POOPSIE.   **Hear ye, hear ye. This way for the knife-throwing exhibition.**
                              BABE *is standing* D.L. *as* PREZ *and* BRENDA *exit*. SID *crosses down*
                              to R. *of her.*
SID.   **Well, if it isn't Miss Grievance Committee.**
BABE.   **Oh, hello.**
SID.   **I have a grievance, there is a new fellow here named Sid Sorokin, been
       knocking himself out trying to be a dandy fellow, but he can't make a
       score.**
                              GROUP *re-forms*, D.R. *for picture taking.*
MAE [*In picture group*].   **Say, Eddie, I want an enlargement of this.**
BABE.   **You tell him Miss Williams is a very cold, hard-boiled doll, and he
        wouldn't like her at all if he got to know her.**
                              GIRL *screams offstage and runs on* L.2. *crosses to* D.R. *and exits.*
                              She is chased by BOY. *Two other* COUPLES *follow them.*
SID.   **I'll tell him but he's an awful problem—stubborn as hell.**
BRENDA [*Rushes in* D.L., *dishevelled*].   **No, I don't. Some people have no sense
        at all, darn fool.**
BABE.   **What happened to you?**
BRENDA.   **Stay out in the open, honey. Don't get down in them woods.** [*Tucks
          in blouse, crosses through groups to* U.R.]
SALESMAN [*Standing* C.]   **Now, hurry, hurry. Make way for the old Professor.**
                              CROWD *ad libs. quietly.*
HINES [*Crosses* D.L. *carrying small table with knives on it*].   **Wait until I place my
       knives.**
SALESMAN.   **Hurry, hurry, hurry for a riot of thrills. Introducing Professor
            Vernon Hines, Master of the Flying Blades . . .**
                              Warn Knife Effect.

CROWD.   **Hurrah!**
                              PREZ *runs on from* U.L.—*stands on table* L.
SALESMAN [*Circling* L. *to* U.L.C.].   **. . . in his sensational demonstration of iron
            nerve and skill exactly as performed in his professional appearance
            before the crowned heads of Missouri and Kansas.**
CROWD.   **Hurrah!** [*Applause.*]
SALESMAN.   **Are you ready, Professor?**
HINES.   **I am ready. Say, is the trained nurse in attendance?**
SALESMAN.   **The trained nurse is here.**
HINES.   **The excitement may prove to be too great a strain on some of our
         fair spectators.**
                              POOPSIE, *standing on table* R., *pretends to swoon in* BOY'S *arms.*

POOPSIE.   **Ooh!**
                              CROWD *laughs.*
HINES [*With knives in hand prepared to make a throw*].   **Ladies and gents, your kind
       attention. Here we go. One—two—three . . .** [*He throws knife . . .Clunk.*]
CROWD.   **Hurrah! Bravo! . . .** [*Applause.*]
                              GIRL *crosses to front of target, and points to where she wants* HINES
                              *to throw the next knife—*BRENDA *pulls her away.*
HINES.   **Get back! Here we go. Ein—zwei—drei . . .** [*Throws second knife . . .
         Clunk. Walking* D.L.] **Now if some daring young lady in the audience will
         consent to stand against the board, I will show you the act as it should be
         played.**
                              CROWD *ad libs agreement and disagreement.*
BRENDA [*In general ad lib*].   **No, Hineszie . . . we all want to live.** [*Moves to
        MAE, who is sitting at table* R.] **You do it, Mae . . . You're so thin he can't
        miss.**
                              CROWD *ad libs.* BRENDA *pulls* MAE *to* C. HINES *pokes* MAE *with*
                              knife. MAE *turns on him furiously as he crosses away* D.L.
MAE.   **Oh, Hineszie, Hineszie!** [*Returns to stool and sits.*]
HINES.   **Eleven years in the public eye and never drew a drop of blood.**
SINGING GIRL I [*From* D.L.].   **Hey Hineszie, I'll do it . . . I'll do it.**
SID [*From* D.L. *taking hold of the* GIRL].   **Hey, hey, don't get foolish.**
BABE [*From* D.R.].   **I'll do it.**

CROWD. **Oh no, Babe, etc., etc.** [*Ad lib.*]

MABEL [*Stepping forward—in general ad lib*]. **Don't be silly, Babe!**

BABE crosses to target and puts apple on her head.

BABE. **Can you knock the apple off my head, Hineszie?** [*Ad libs "William Tell" overture.*]

PREZ. **That's the spirit Babe . . . you show 'em, kid! ! '**

CROWD *ad libs*

MABEL. **I don't think she should.**

GLADYS. **No, she shouldn't.**

SINGING GIRL II. **No, no, no.**

HINES [*Quietening crowd*]. **Hold still! And you won't get hurt! One—two— three . . .**

HINES *throws knife . . . Clunk.* CROWD *ad libs.* BABE *ducks. The apple rolls to* C. *She runs to get it, but* SID *gets it first.*

BABE. **Where's my apple?**

SID. **I think that's enough!**

BABE. **Give it to me.**

[*Covered by* CROWD *noise.*]

BABE *gets the apple from* SID *and returns to target.*

BRENDA [*Crossing to R. of* HINES D.L.]. **Hineszie! Hineszie! You're making us all so nervous!**

HINES. **Making you nervous? How the hell do you think I feel?**

POOPSIE. **She's shaking . . . My God, she's shaking!**

BRENDA. **You'd better not, Babe!**

MAE. **Something awful is going to happen.**

[CROWD *ad libs quietly.*]

SID. **Come on now! Don't be a damned fool!**

BABE. **Keep out of this. Go on, shoot, Professor!**

CROWD *ad libs.*

HINES. **Now just relax. Quiet, everybody, quiet.** [*Stamping foot angrily— facing around—back to audience.*] **Hold still! One—two—three . . .** [*Throws knife . . . Clunk.*]

CROWD *gasps and screams.*

MABEL. **Is it over? Oooohhh! ! ! !** [*She collapses in a dead faint stage* C. *Falls on* BOY.]

SID [*Crosses to* BABE, *pushes her* C., *and breaks up the crowd*]. **Now cut it out! Get those tables out of here! Damn it, break it up! ! ! !** [*Crosses to* HINES *and grabs him.*]

The CROWD *breaks up and exits, clearing tables, target, card table, benches, stools. etc., as they leave. The two trestle tables, cleared of bottles, etc., are left half onstage for the dance which follows.*

HINES. **It's an insult. My skill has never been questioned before.**

SID. **Oh, go drown yourself.** [*Crosses* R. *and helps carry* MABEL *off* D.R.]

DANCING GIRL [*Enters from* D.R.]. **Hey, kids. Guess what? Mr. Hasler's playing first base, and he's so funny.** [*Exits* D.R.]

BRENDA. **Hasler? First base? Holy smoke. Let's go.**

Exits D.R. *with* GIRL.

HINES [*To* GLADYS]. **I tell you, I'm not jealous.**

GLADYS. **I didn't say you were jealous, I said you were drunk.**

HINES. **Well, you can't have everything.**

HINES *exits* D.L. *with his knife table, following* GLADYS. *There is a general ad lib as remainder of* CROWD *disperses off stage.* PREZ *crosses to* L. *of* MAE, *who is* C. *backing to* L.C.

PREZ [*Steps* D.S. *from behind tree* L.]. **Where are you going, Mae?**

MAE. **No place special.**

PREZ *nods head off* L —*pulls her off* L. *by arm.* BABE *is left on stage alone, standing* C. SID *enters* D.R., *and crosses to* BABE.

SID. **My, but you're an impetuous girl.**

Warn Cue 23

BABE. **I get along all right.**

SID. **That defiant policy of yours is going to get you into trouble some day, Catherine Williams.**

BABE. **Well, it's been working out all right so far.**

SID. **Listen, I've got a new policy in mind. For both you and me.**

BABE. **Oh?**

SID. **Let's quit fighting.**

BABE. **What fight?**

SID. **Come here, Catherine.**

Music No. 10. **" ONCE-A-YEAR DAY "** (*and Polka*)

SID *takes* BABE's *hand and leads her to* D.R.

BABE [*Spoken*]. **Where are we going?**

SID [*Spoken*]. **Babe and Sid are going for a walk together. The new policy, Babe.** [*He backs her up against a tree. They kiss.*] **Gee, baby . . . you're terrific.** [*He takes her hand.*]

BABE [*Spoken. Facing him — holding his* U.S. *hand, patting his* D.S. *shoulder*]. **You're not so bad yourself . . .** [*They cross to* C.]

Cue 23

SID [*Sings*].   THIS is my once-a-year-day,
Once-a-year-day
Felt the morning sun and knew that
This was my once-a-year-day,
Once-a-year-day.
Even got a kiss from you,   [*Turns* BABE *round.*]
I feel like hoppin' up and down,
[*Lifts* BABE *up—she kicks her feet in the air.*]
Like a kangaroo,
Jumpin' fences, climbin' trees,
What pleases me is what I'll do
'Cause

QUARTET [3 BOYS, 1 GIRL].   This is our once-a-year-day,
Once-a-year-day.
Everyone's entitled to be wild,
Be a child, be a goof, raise the roof
Once a year!

ALL.   This is our once-a-year-day,
Once-a-year-day,
Once a year we're jumpin' fences,
This is our once-a-year-day,

> GIRL *and* BOY *cross to* R.C.—*he holds her feet—she walks on hands—* BABE *watches—edges* R. *after them.*

Once-a-year-day,
Once a year we lose our senses,

> BABE *crossing* R.C.

BABE.   Look at Charlie up a tree
Kissin' Katie's ear,
Charlie's wife is mad as hell!

ALL   Oh well, it happens once-a-year.

> BABE *and* SID *exit* D.R.

And this is that one-a-year-day,
Once-a-year-day,

> 3 DANCING BOYS *do leap-frog across stage.*

Everyone's entitled to be wild,
Be a child, be a goof, raise the roof
Once a year!

POOPSIE.   Look at Papa Halterbush,
Ninety-two today,
Running off with Sadie Lee

ALL.   He's heading for that pile of hay,
'Cause
This is his once-a-year day,
Once-a-year-day,
Everyone's entitled to be wild,
Be a child, be a goof, raise the roof
Once a year!

> POOPSIE *exits* D.R.
> *Dance.*
> *When* DANCING BOYS *leap off tables*—Warn Cues 24 and 25, Limes and Flys.
> *At end of dance they all fall down.* GLADYS *and* DANCING BOYS *pop up as lights black out.*
> *When* GLADYS *and* DANCING BOYS *pop up*—Cue 24, Limes out.
> *When lights out*—Picnic Gauze and Black drop in.
> *When Picnic Gauze in*—Cue 25.

ACT I—SCENE 7. PICNIC CROSSOVER

> *It is twilight. The setting is the same as for Scene 5.*
> SALESMAN, MABEL *and* CHARLIE *enter* D.R. *and cross* L.

SALESMAN [*Crosses to* L.]. **Sounds gruesome to me.**

MABEL [*Crosses to* L.C.]. **That ain't the worst of it.** [*Stops, turns to look at* CHARLIE, *who has also stopped.*] **Come on, Charlie . . . If I can make it, you can.**

[*Crosses to* R. *of* SALESMAN *who has stopped* D.L.] **Well anyway he was Elsie
Bartlett's second cousin. He fell into the concrete mixer when they were
building the new bridge.**
CHARLIE. **My God!**
MABEL. **They never did find the body, so they poured the concrete and held
the funeral on top of the second pier on the Illinois side.**

ALL EXIT *slowly* D.L.

Music No. 10A. " ONCE-A-YEAR-DAY " *Crossover*

Groups of weary BOYS *and* GIRLS *supporting each other cross* R. *to* L.
singing a slow version of " Once-A-Year Day ". 1ST HELPER
sings " Be a goof "—tips bottle over—drinks. They all cross to
D.L. *and exit.*
PREZ *and* MAE *enter from* D.R., *cross to* R.C.

MAE. **What I like about picnics . . . they bring people together.**
PREZ. **They sure do.**
MAE. **I never thought you was aware I was alive until today.**
PREZ. **How could I miss you. You're the kind that stands out in a crowd.
You know what I mean? You've got what it takes. You know something
else . . . that's a mighty elegant outfit you got on.**
MAE. **Oh, it's just casual.** [*Crosses to* L. *below* PREZ.]

PREZ *tries to kiss her. She pushes him away, sending him hurtling
to the ground.*

Listen, Prez . . . what would your wife say?
PREZ. [*Picking himself up*]. **Don't worry about that.** [*Crossing to* R. *of her.*] **Her
and me hardly talk to each other any more.**
MAE. **You don't?**
PREZ. **Certainly not.**
MAE. **You know what? Something I like about you.** [SHE *punches him in the
stomach with her elbow.*] **You got such a swell brain.**
PREZ. [*Gulping*]. **So have you.**
MAE. **You're a snappy dresser too.**
PREZ. **Oh, I get around.**
MAE. **I go for that.**
PREZ. **I go for you.**
MAE. **Ha, Ha, Ha.**
PREZ. **Ha, Ha, Ha.**

Music No. 11. " HER IS " (*Reprise*)

PREZ [*Sings*].   **Her is a kinda doll what drives a fellow bats,
Isn't her?**
MAE [*Sings. Hands on hips*].
Her is.
PREZ.   **Her has the kinda shape** [*Indicates her figure.*]
**What really is the cats,
Hasn't her?**
MAE [*Hands back of head*].
Her has.
PREZ.   **I've seen what girls East to the West have,
None have what her has,** [*Jabs her* R. *hip with finger.*]
**Yes, I have seen what the best have.
But you have
Twice as much as the rest have.**

MAE *dances, imitating* GLADYS, R. *to* L.

Warn Cues 26 and 27, Sound, Limes and
Flys.

**Her is a snappy dresser what is dressed to kill,
Isn't her?**
MAE.   **Her is!**
PREZ.   **Her is the only doll from which I get a thrill,**
MAE *turns sexily.*
Isn't her?
MAE.   **Her is.**   THEY *start dancing off* L.
PREZ [*Crossing* L.] **Her is running away
But her sure can bet
Him is gonna get her yet,
I'm gonna get her yet!**

THEY *exit.*
As MAE *yanks* PREZ *off* L.—Cue. 26. Limes Out.
When lights out—Picnic Gauze and Black Drop Away.
When Picnic Gauze 12 *ft. high*—Train Whistle Go, Cue. 27.

ACT I—SCENE 8.   THE KITCHEN OF BABE'S HOUSE

D.S.R. is a table with a coffee cup on it, and two chairs set one at either end. SID is seated on the R. chair, POP is on the L. chair. There are low fitted cupboards running along most of the wall area from R. to L. D.S.R., on the cupboard is an upright-type telephone. The back wall is broken by two windows on either side of a central door. Under the R. window is a stove, with pots and pans, etc., hanging near. Under the L. window is the sink. To the left of the sink is a large refrigerator. D.S. of the refrigerator is a door leading off to the rest of the house. D.S.L. is a Morris-type chair on a small rug. U.S. of the chair is a small occasional table with papers on it. We can see the night sky above the house, and the trellis-work of railway signal lights.

POP.   When you first come here after that picnic last week, she says to me . . . don't be a pest . . . don't talk too damned much. [*He laughs.*] But it might be worse if I didn't talk at all, eh, Sid?

SID.   You're right.

POP.   I always say a railroad man can't be too much of a damned pest 'cause he ain't home enough.

SID [*Laughs politely*].   You go out on your run tonight, don't you?

POP.   Yes . . . off to Milwaukee doggone it! [*Taking petrified bat out of his pocket.*] Say, here's something you don't see every day. [*Leans over table.*]

SID.   I agree.   What is it?

POP.   A petrified bat.

BABE enters from bedroom L.—slams door loudly—crosses to L.C.

BABE.   Now, Pop, Sid is not interested in petrified bats.

POP [*Rises—crosses to C.*].   Well, what the hell, dear . . . I didn't say he was.

BABE.   I know you.

POP [*Crosses towards bedroom door below Morris chair*].   The tyranny of women.

BABE.   Too bad.

POP.   Well, I'd better get my things. [*Takes watch out.*] Old number fifteen waits for no man.

POP exits into bedroom. BABE crosses to chair L. of table—kneels on it, pulling it slightly U.S. as she does so.

BABE.   Pop belt your ears off?

SID.   He's a great guy . . . I like him.   But I like you better. [*He rises . . . goes to her and tries to kiss her.*]

BABE [*Pulls away—steps D.C.—faces front*].   No, no, no.   Wait till Pop goes out.

BABE turns away from him and crosses C.

Are you hungry? [*Crosses to ice-box U.L.*]

SID [*Follows her to ice-box and kisses her neck at end of speech*].   Not exactly hungry. Not the way you mean anyway.

BABE.   Oh you. [*He tries to kiss her again. She pushes him away and hands him a bottle of beer.*] Here, have a beer.

SID.   Thanks.

Warn sound.

BABE crosses to stove U.R. SID is above Morris chair. POP enters from bedroom, carrying his stamp album. He crosses to L. of SID.

POP.   Say, Sid.   You like stamps?

BABE.   Pop! ! !

BABE bangs down kitchen pan on stove.

POP.   Well, even if he don't this is something that should be interesting to anybody. [*He hands album to SID. Crosses to U.C., gets his lunch pail from sink, then crosses to BABE.*] Two sets of Mint Columbians.   Plate blocks on every issue since 1919.

SID.   Well thanks.

POP.   Goodbye, Katie. [*Kisses BABE, crosses to door C.*]

BABE.   Goodbye.

POP.   Come around any time, Sid.

Train whistle go.

SID.   I'd like to.

POP exits. SID takes off coat—puts it on Morris chair. Crosses round chair with album, and sits.

Well now we can settle down for a nice long evening with the stamp album. [*He looks at album.*] Say, he has got a full set of Mint Columbians.

BABE [*She crosses to ice-box and then back of SID's chair and puts her hands on his shoulders*].   Sure he has.   That's why I work at Sleep Tite.

SID.   He's a nice guy, Babe. [*Closes album, puts it on small table U.S. of chair.*]

BABE.   You're a good boy, Sid.   He likes you too.

SID [*Kisses her hand*].   I feel good, Babe.   I feel like home.

BABE [*Smiles at him, then raises her head slightly*].   I wonder if we've got any onions.

SID. **Onions?**

Warn Cue 28.

BABE [*She crosses to ice-box*].   **I'm gonna make a sandwich. Want one?**

SID.   **That's my baby, boys. She wants a sandwich.**

BABE *crosses to stove.*

No, honey, I do not want a sandwich. [*He rises and crosses to* L. *end of kitchen table.*] **Food is not uppermost in my thoughts at the moment.**

BABE [*She crosses down to* R. *end of kitchen table, putting cup and saucer on table.*] **Guess you'll want some coffee too.**

SID.   **No . . . it'll keep me awake. Now cut it out.** [*Crosses* R. *to above table.*]

Music No. 12.   " SMALL TALK "

BABE.   **What's the matter, lover?**

SID [*Sings*].   **I DON'T wanna talk small talk** [*At back of table.*]

Cue 28.

Now that I'm alone with you.

BABE *fixes his tie.*

I don't wanna talk small talk, [*Leaning over chair.*]
We've got bigger things to do.

BABE *crosses below table. Slowly.*

Let's not talk of the weather,
Or the fashions for the fall.
[*Crosses, around table to* L.C. *Slowly to her* L.]
Why don't you stop all this small talk?
I've got something better for your lips to do,
[*Arms around her waist.*]
And that takes no talk at all.
[*Leans forward to kiss her.*]

BABE.   **I gotta buy me a dressy dress,**
The one I have is such a mess!

SID.   **Small talk!** [*Walks away* C. *and comes back.*]

BABE [*Sits up from table and stops him*].

Who will you vo e for next election?
How do you likethe stamp collection?

SID.   **Small talk!**

BABE *sits on table and* SID *leans on it.*

Read in a book the other day
That halibut spawn in early May,
And horses whinny and donkeys bray
And furthermore [*Step* L.]
The pygmy tribes in Africa may
Have a war.

BABE [*Spoken*].   **No?** [*She turns, picks up paper off table.*]

SID [*Spoken*].   **Yes!**

[*Sings.*]   **I don't**

BABE *crosses* L.—SID *follows, crossing* R. *all around table.*
SID *holds her.*

Wanna talk small talk.

BABE [*Sings*].   **What do you think they charge for ham now?**

SID.   **Now that I'm alone with you.** [*Crosses to* C.]

BABE.   **Got so a buck ain't worth a damn now.**

SID.   **I don't want to talk small talk.**

BABE.   **Read where the Winters are getting milder.** [*Turns.*]

SID.   **We've bigger things to do.** [*He closes in, tries to hold her.*]

BABE [*Holds paper up*].

And that the teen-age kids are wilder.

SID.   **Let's not talk of the weather,** [*Takes paper from her, folds it and throws on Morris chair.*]

BABE [*Breaks to* C. *facing* R.].

One of these days I'll paint the kitchen,

Warn Cue 29.

SID [*Puts arms around her*].

Or the fashions for the fall.

BABE.   **Get Pop to put a new light switch in.**

SID [*Backing her to table*].

Why don't you stop all this small talk? [*He holds her.*]

BABE.   **Like I was sayin'**

SID.   **I've got something better**

BABE.   **What I mean is**

SID.   For your lips.

BABE.   I was only

SID.   To do. [*Spoken.*] And that TAKES no talk at all!

Cue 29.

THEY *kiss on this phrase. Music continues under dialogue.*

BABE [*Spoken*]. **I think I'll make that sandwich.** [*Crosses up* L.C. *to drawer under sink, searches through cloths in it.*]

SID. **Oh, Babe,** [*Following to* L. *of her.*] **have a heart.**

BABE [*Closes drawer*]. **Every darned apron in the wash.** [*Crosses* D.C.]

SID [*Comes* D.C.]. **That's your great worry in life, eh?**

BABE. **I don't want to get grease spots on this dress. I paid twenty bucks for it.**

SID. **Take it off.** [*Moves to her.*] **You're among friends.** [*He starts to embrace her.*]

BABE. **Look out, I'm cooking.**

SID. **You sure are.**

THEY *kiss.* BOTH *sit in chair* L. *of table.* BABE *rises and walks away from* SID.

BABE. **Well, I might as well be practical.** [*Takes belt off—crosses* U.R. *back of table, puts belt on it. She takes her dress off.*] **Would you hang it up for me, please?** [*Hands dress to* SID.]

SID *starts across stage* L. *with dress in hand—stops* L.C.*—turns to look at her.* BABE *crosses up to stove.*

SID. **Gee! I love to see a girl wandering around the house in her slip.** [BABE *stands still above table.*] **If I was an Oriental potentate I'd have the girls in the harem parading around in slips instead of those damn pants.** [*Crosses to hanger* D.L.*—*BABE *rolls up belt and puts it on cabinet* D.R.*—*SID *fumbles with her dress and hanger.*] **How the hell do you hang this thing up?**

BABE. **Keep trying, lover.**

SID *hangs it up, and puts his own coat with it.*

SID. **I got it. Sport coat . . . this is Miss Williams' dress. You two kids get acquainted.**

BABE *is standing by the table looking at him.* SID *looks at her and suddenly his mood changes.*

Babe, I love you

Music fades.
BABE *sits on* L. *chair.* SID *goes and kneels beside her. They embrace.*

SID. **Darling.**

BABE. **Sid. There's something I got to talk about.**

SID. **What?**

BABE. **I think you're wonderful and I love you. But we're in for a lot of trouble.**

SID. **No, baby, why should we be?**

BABE [*Rises, crosses* L. *to* D.S. *of Morris chair*]. **There's something going to come between us.**

SID. **Who?**

BABE [*Turns to him*]. **Not any who. Seven-and-a-half cents.**

SID [*Rises, crosses to* L.C.]. **Oh, that!**

BABE. **That contract, lover . . . that's important. Maybe we ought to** *FACE* **that before . . .**

SID. **Don't talk nonsense.** [*He tries to kiss her, but she struggles away.*]

BABE [*To above chair* L.]. **You mustn't treat me like a baby**

SID. **I'm not darling.**

Warn Cues, 30 and 30a, Flys.

BABE. **You've got to listen. I don't know why the Union's so important to me . . . but it is . . .I guess you got to be on a team. And that's why no matter what's with us . . . I'm going to be fighting for my side and fighting hard.**

SID. **All right.** [*Pause.*] **How do you feel about me, Babe?**

Music re-commences.

BABE [*Pause*]. **I love you terribly.**

SID [*Kneels on Morris chair*]. **If we both feel that way about each other, isn't that enough?**

BABE. **You don't know me.**

SID. **Babe, I love you.**

BABE. **All right. I can take it if you can.**

[*Crossing to him, sings.*] **I don't wanna talk small talk.** [*Embraces him.*]

SID [*Sings*].   **I've got something better for your lips to do, And that takes no talk at all.**

THEY *kiss and sit in chair.*
When they are nearly seated—Cue 30.
When lights out and truck U.S.*—Elevator Cloth in.*
When elevator cloth in—Cue 30a

The setting is the same as in Scene 3. As the lights come on, PREZ, POOPSIE, MAE, 2ND HELPER and BRENDA enter from D.L., and cross to R.C.

PREZ.   Mr. Hasler called. I spoke to him personally. He says he wants to see us tomorrow in his office at noon.

POOPSIE.   Does that mean we've won?

MAE.   We've won. We've won. Hurray.

MAE grabs the 2ND HELPER and jumps up and down with him, nearly breaking him in two. When she releases him he doubles up in pain, and staggers D.R.

Oh, I'm sorry.

PREZ.   Take it easy, Mae. Mr. Hasler just wants to talk to us.

BRENDA.   Shouldn't we wait for Babe?

POOPSIE.   What for? You know who she's going out with . . . Mr. Somebody Special.

BRENDA.   Babe's all right.

POOPSIE.   I didn't say she wasn't, but she sure is busy these days.

MAE.   I don't think a girl should get too emotional over the management.

BRENDA.   Babe can take care of herself.

MAE [*Looks at* PREZ *and back to* BRENDA].   The trouble is when you start falling for a guy, how do you know how far you're going to fall?

Music No. 12A.   " I'M NOT AT ALL IN LOVE "   (Incidental)

BABE enters from D.L.

BRENDA.   Hello, Babe. We're talkin' about you.

BABE.   Why not?

BRENDA.   Are you coming?

BABE.   No, I've got a date.

BRENDA.   Have fun.

BABE.   I will.

THEY all exit D.R., leaving BABE alone on the stage. BABE turns L. and says:

Here I am! Hi!

SID enters from D.L. and crosses to her at C.

SID.   Hi! Did I keep you waiting?

BABE.   That makes it much nicer when you got here.

SID.   I've got one more thing to do! Do you mind another five minutes?

BABE.   I don't mind anything. I love you.

SID.   I love you more. [*Pause. He puts arm around her. They cross to R.*] Babe, are you happy?

Music stops.

BABE.   I don't even touch the ground.

SID.   It's good, isn't it?

Warn Cue 30b.

BABE.   So good I can hardly believe it. Tell me.

SID.   Again? [*Backing away from her.*]

BABE.   Tell me.

SID.   I love you.

BABE.   Tell me.

SID.   I love you more than all the heroes in all the history books in the world.

BABE.   Tell me.

SID.   What a woman. I'll tell you.

Music No. 13.   " THERE ONCE WAS A MAN "

SID signals for BABE to come to him. She does so and sits on his knee.

[*Sings.*]   THERE once was a man who loved a woman,

Cue 30b.

She was the one he slew the dragon for!
They say that nobody ever loved as much as he-ee,
But me-ee, [*Kiss.*] I love you more.

BABE [*Spoken*].   Tell me!

SID [*Sings*].   And there was once a man, who loved a woman.
She was the one he gave his kingdom for.
They say that nobody ever loved as much as he-ee.
But me-ee, [*Kiss.*] I love you more!
My love is a giant, fierce and defiant,
But how can I prove it to you?
Ain't got no kingdom, no dragon, to back up my braggin'.
How can I show what I would do?
I only know, there once was a man, who loved a woman,

	She was the one he ate the apple for,
	They say that nobody ever loved as much as he-ee,
	But me-ee, I love you more!
BABE [*Sings*.]	There once was a woman, who loved a man,
	He was the one that she took poison for!
	They say that nobody ever loved as much as she-ee,
	But me-ee, I love you more!
	And there once was a woman, who loved a man.
	He was the one she swam the Channel for.
	They say that nobody ever loved as much as she-ee,
	But me-ee, I love you more!
	My love's meteoric, it's merely historic,
	A whirlwind, a cyclone on wheels!
	It rocks 'muh' whole solar plexus, it's bigger 'n Texas.
	I just can't tell you how it feels!
	I only know, there once was a woman, who loved a man.
	Loved him enough to cause the Trojan War.
	They say that nobody ever loved as much as she-ee,
	But me-ee, I love you more! More! More! More!

Warn Cues 30c, and 33, Flys.

SID.	More than a hangman loves his rope,
BABE.	More than a dope-fiend loves his dope,
SID.	More than an Injun loves his scalps,
BABE.	More than a yodeller loves his Alps.

SID. **More.** BABE. **More.** SID. **More.** BABE. **More.** SID. **More.** BABE. **More.**

SID.	**More.**
	There once was a man who loved a woman.
BABE.	There once was a woman who loved a man.
SID.	She was the one he slew the dragon for!
BABE.	He was the one that she took poison for!
BOTH.	They say that nobody ever loved as much as he-ee/she-ee,
	But me-ee, I love you more!
	But me-ee, I love you more!

BABE *jumps into* SID'S *arms and is carried off* D.L.
As they exit—Cue 30c.
When lights out—Elevator Cloth away.
When elevator cloth away—Cue 33.

ACT I—SCENE 10.   THE FACTORY

*The setting is the same as in Scene 2. When the lights come on we
see four* GIRLS *standing above machines* U.L. BRENDA *and* POOPSIE
are standing U.R., *listening off* R. MABEL *enters* D.R., *crosses to* C.,
then sees BRENDA *and* POOPSIE.

MABEL. **Well.**
BRENDA [*To* R. *of* MABEL].   **The committee is in there, talking to Mr. Hasler
      right now.**
MABEL [*Crossing to* L.C.].   **I'm steering clear of there. I'll go get my lunch.**
BRENDA.   **We ate already.**

POOPSIE *and* BRENDA *exit* D.L., *keeping* U.S. *of* MABEL. MABEL
crosses to L. *and meets* BABE, *who enters from* D.L.

MABEL.   **Well, Babe.**
BABE.   **Howdy, Mabel.**
MABEL.   **I hear you and Sid make a lovely couple on the dance floor.** [*Exits* D.L.]

PREZ, MAE *and* JOE *enter from* U.R. *and cross to* C.

PREZ.   **Sure thing.**
MAE.   **I told you we wouldn't get no place.**
JOE.   **Looks like another run-around, Prez.** [*Crosses back of* PREZ *to* L.]
PREZ [*Turning to* MAE].   **He's a fighter, he says. What a line.** [*Turns to* BABE.]
MAE.   **You should have heard him, Babe.**

GLADYS *enters from* U.R., *and crosses to* R.C. *As she speaks the*
FOUR GIRLS U.S. *of machines exit* U.L.

GLADYS.   **Wait a minute please. Mr. Hasler wants to speak to you again.**
MAE.   **More soft soap.** [*Crosses to* L. *of* PREZ.]
PREZ.   **Now, Mae, quiet down.**

HASLER *enters from* U.R., *crosses down to* R. *of* PREZ.

HASLER.   **I just want to add one thought. Let's not adjourn with any hard
      feelings. We want to preserve that fine Sleep Tite spirit.**
PREZ.   **That's easy to say, Mr. Hasler, but we're not getting any place.**
MAE.   **We're goin' backwards.**

Warn Sound.

HASLER. I didn't say no. I said not NOW.

PREZ. Look Mr. Hasler, this thing's been draggin' on for months. The help are getting very jumpy. Their patience is about wore out.

HASLER. I want to be fair but . . .

PREZ. I'm going to tell you the plain truth. We know the company is doin' one hell of a business. We don't have no education maybe, but we got eyes and ears.

MAE. Everybody in the industry has had a seven-and-a-half cents raise but us.

HASLER. As I said, I want to be fair. That's always been my policy. So I don't give you a yes and I don't give you a no. I say we've got to examine it . . . and I've got to talk to the board and that's the way we're going to leave it.

HASLER *exits* U.R., *followed by* GLADYS.

MAE. **What now, Prez?**

PREZ [*Pause*]. **Slow down!**

MAE. **Atta boy. This is it.**

Gong go.

There's the bell.

GIRLS *start entering from* U.L., *and* D.L., BRENDA *enters from* D.L. *They all go to their machines.* MAE, *crossing* L. *to* BABE.

This is what we've been waiting for.

JOE. **We got to get started some place.** [*Exits* D.L.]

PREZ [*To* BRENDA *as she passes him*]. **Slow down.** [*He crosses to* BABE.] **You're in charge of this room, Babe. Go to it.** [*He starts out* L.] **Slow down!**

PREZ *exits* D.L. *They all pass the word from one to the other as they resume their places at the machines. After the girls are set,* BABE *crosses to the third machine and tells* GIRL *she will take her place.* GIRL *rises and runs off* D.R. BABE *takes her place at the sewing machine. The Music begins.*

Music No. 14. FACTORY MUSIC

During this introductory music the GIRLS *go about their business very slowly and laboriously.* HINES *enters from* U.R. *He crosses to* C., *and tries to take pajama trousers from* GIRL *who is slowly moving them from* L. *to* R. *He misses them and nearly falls over. He pulls a stop-watch from his pocket, beats a faster tempo with his foot and says:*

HINES. **Something's very wrong here.** [*Crosses up to* POOPSIE *who is slowly lifting a bobbin off top tray. He helps her to lift it down.*] **What's the matter?**

POOPSIE. **I guess I'm just overworked or something, Mr. Hines. Ever since lunch I just can't seem to get the hang of it.**

HINES. **Well, I think I got the hang of it and I'm going to see the superintendent on what's going on around here.**

HINES *exits* U.R.

BOYS *and* GIRLS *enter* R. *and* L.

Music No. 14A. SLOW DOWN

GIRLS I [*Singing slow-down version*].

   Hurry up, hurry up, hurry up, hurry up,

GIRLS II. **Can't waste time, can't waste time,**

   Hurry up, hurry up, hurry up, hurry up,

GIRLS III. **Can't waste time, can't waste time.**

GIRLS I. **When you're racing with the clock,**

   When you're racing with the clock,

GIRLS I AND III. **And the second hand doesn't understand**

ALL GIRLS. **That your back may break and your fingers ache,**

SID *enters with* HINES *from* U.R. *They cross to* U.C.

And your constitution isn't made of rock. [*They stop suddenly.*]

Warn Sound.

SID. **All right, girls. Just a minute. Now listen to me. This is a nice little show you're putting on here but I don't like it.** [*Crosses to* L.] **My job is to turn out goods and that's what we're gonna do.** [*Crosses to* C.] **You have a contract, I didn't make it but it's there.** [*Looks* L. *at girls at bench.*] **I want a day's work for a day's pay.** [*Looks at girls* D.R.] **I can still hire and fire around here, you know.** [*Crosses back to* C.] **Now let's go!**

Music No. 14B. FACTORY MUSIC

The work is resumed at normal tempo. SID *turns away from girls at machines and looks at* GIRLS *standing* R.C.—*then* D.R.—*then*

> D.L.—*then moves* U.C.—*as he does so,* BABE *rises from her chair,*
> *makes up her mind and then sits down again, kicking her foot into*
> *the machinery as she does so.*
> *Music stops.*   Crash go.
> *This causes a breakdown of the entire line. A loud sound of grinding*
> *gears is heard.* SID *turns to the* GIRLS *at the machines.* BABE *is*
> *now standing.*

HINES.   **Somebody jammed the line**

SID.   **Who did that?**

BABE.   **I did.**

SID.   **You're fired.**

BABE.   **I am?**

SID.   **Yes.**

BABE.   **That's fine. First vacation I've had in three years. I need one.** [*Starts*
to exit D.L.] **So long, girls.**

> Warn Cue 35 and House Tabs.

> BABE *exits* D.L.

SID [*To* BOY, *who is* D.L.] **Get Charlie. We'll be operating again in fifteen**
minutes. Now clear out till I call you back.

> *Music No. 15.*   **FINALE—ACT I**

> ALL *exit* L. *and* R.   SID *crosses to broken machine.* CHARLIE *enters*
> *from* U.L. *with switch.*

CHARLIE.   **I've got a fuse and a switch.** [*Crosses to* C.]

> *The machine* SID *is working at suddenly explodes.* (*Note:* SID
> *operates a switch under the bench to cause the explosion.*)

Boy! Look out. Didja get burnt!

> SID *has jumped back from the machine. He is* D.C.

SID.   **Yeah.** [*Looks off in the direction which* BABE *has gone.*] **Twice.**

CHARLIE.   **I'll fix it.**

> CHARLIE *crosses to machine and begins working on it.* SID *crosses*
> *to* D.C. *Looks off* L. *and sings.*
> Cue 35.

SID.   Better forget her,
              Her with her nose in the air,
              She had you dancing on a string,
              Break it and she won't care.
              Will you take this advice I hand you like a brother?
              Or are you not seeing things too clear,
              Are you just too far gone to hear,
              Is it all going in one ear
              And out the other?

> *On* " *Other* "—House Tabs in medium.
> *When House Tabs in*—House Lights on.

INTERVAL

Pre-Set	..	..	..	..	..	House Tabs in. Scene I lighting on. Eagle flat in. Grey drop in. Panels Clear.
1 min. before Entracte	..	..	..	..		Send M.D. in.
Start of Entracte	..	..	..	..		3 Bar-bells. No. 1 and 2 Bat. Pilots off. Check following — " Steam-Heat " on Stage. PREZ Stage R.
Entracte	..	..	..	..	..	" I'll never be jealous again," " Small Talk," " Once-a-Year Day," " Hey There," " I'm Not at all in Love ".
End of " Hey There " in Entracte		..	..			House Lights out.
End of Entracte, Applause	..	..	..			House Tabs up.

SCENE I. EAGLE HALL

Music No. 16A. OPENING, ACT II

As Curtain rises PREZ *enters from D.R.* GLADYS *and* TWO *"Steam Heat"* BOYS *are standing behind the Eagle Flat on stage.*

PREZ [*Crosses to* C.]. **This is just going to be a short meeting because the Boiler-Makers Local is got the hall spoke for at eight o'clock. So, them that wants to get over to the Tri-State Meet will have plenty of time.** [*Hands in pockets.*] **What's going on down to the plant you all know as good as I.** [*Hands out of pockets, points to himself.*] **And any members of the type I run into from time to time who say " What good is the Union, why should I pay my dues?" why they could get a mighty good object-lesson from where would they be now in this here battle for seven-and-a-half cents that they wouldn't get if it wasn't for the union—** [*Pounds fist into hand.*] **what sure as hell's going to get it.** [*Puts up hands to stop applause.*]

Warn Cue 1a and Flys.

So leave us all remember that our union should be first and foremost in our minds, next only to our loved ones and the tiny tots and kiddies. [*Crosses* R.] **Now before we break up we are going to have a little entertainment and I hope you are going to show a special courtesy to-night because a couple of the cutting-room boys has got up an act with Gladys Hotchkiss who's from the front office. And if these good folk is good enough to come down here and do this act for us why the least you can do is not to sneak out the back way, like last time. The little number they worked up is something that's right on the nose because it's about getting hot. And fellow union members that's what we're doing—** [*Motions banner flat up.*] **getting hot!**

PREZ *exits* D.R. Cue 1a. Eagle Flat up.

Music No. 17. " STEAM HEAT "

The Eagle Hall Flat flies out, GLADYS *and " Steam Heat "* BOYS *are discovered standing stage* C.

GLADYS AND BOYS [*Sing. Hats out from chest and back again on end of "steam"*].
    Yeah!
    I got [*Clang*] [*Clang*] **s - s - s - steam heat,**
    I got [*Clang*] [*Clang*] **s - s - s - steam heat,**
    I got [*Clang*] [*Clang*] **s - s - s - steam heat,**
    But I need your love to keep away the cold.

* *The clang is produced in the vocal chorus like a " clack "—the tongue hitting the roof of the mouth.*

    [*Hats on heads—both hands holding—elbow out.*]
    [*Raise hats.*]
    I got [*Clang*] [*Clang*] **s - s - s - steam heat,**
    [*Hats back on heads and go* L.]
    I got [*Clang*] [*Clang*] **s - s - s - steam heat,** [*Go* L.]
    I got [*Clang*] [*Clang*] **s - s - s - steam heat,**
    [*Hats back on heads and go* L.]
    But I can't get warm without your hand to hold!
    [R. *arm high with hat. Moving sideways from* L. *to* C.]
    The radiator's hissin',
    Still I need your kissin',
    To keep me from freezin' each night!
    [*Boom ba. Extra knee clasp.* R. *hand on hat—*L. *down.*]
    I got a hot water bottle [*Hold position.*]
    But nothing I got'll
    Take the place of you, holding me tight
    [R.L. *steps back and embrace self.*]

[*Hat on head.*]

I got [*Clang*] [*Clang*] **s - s - s - steam heat**
[*Arms swing front and back.*]
I got [*Clang*] [*Clang*] **s - s - s - steam heat,** [*As above.*]
I got [*Clang*] [*Clang*] **s - s - s - steam heat,** [*As above.*]
But I need your love to keep away the cold. [*Hats on chest.*]

*Interlude. Hat trick No. 1—*GLADYS*—*BOYS *dance.*

TWO BOYS [*Loose-jointed step from* L. *to* R. *Shoulders up and down, turned-in feet.*]
They told me to shovel more coal in the boiler, [*Business as above.*]
They told me to shovel more coal in the boiler, [*Business as above.*]
They told me to shovel more coal in the boiler, [*Business as above.*]

Warn Cue 1b.

[*On knees all arms front and back.*]

GLADYS [*On knees—*D.S. R.C.].
But that don't do no good. [*On knees all arms front and back.*]
[*Crossing on knees far* L.]

BOYS.   **They told me to pour some more oil in the burner,**
[*Walk on knees* F.]
They told me to pour some more oil in the burner,
[*Crossing on knees to* L.]
They told me to pour some more oil in the burner,
[*Crossing on knees to* L.]

GLADYS.   **But that don't do no good** [*All get up* R.L. *and go down.*]
[*Clap section for all.*]

Cue 1b.

BOYS [*Spoken in rhythm*].   **Coal in the boiler**

Warn Cue 1c, 1d, 2 and 3, Limes, Flys.

GLADYS [*Spoken in rhythm*].   **No good.**
BOYS [*Spoken in rhythm*].   **Oil in the burner**
GLADYS [*Spoken in rhythm*].   **No good.**
ALL   **Cold, No, Hot, Yes, s-s, Yes, Yes, Yes,**
                                Come on union get hot.

Hand-clap rhythm section and 4 steps going to S.R.—*on 2nd four orchestra drums joins—Dance—Drum Section—Dance.*

[*Spoken*].   **Boink, Boink—Boink, Boink—Boink, Boink.**

BOYS [*Sing*].   **I need your love to keep away the cold,**
I need your love to keep away the cold, s - s - s
Yeah!

On Music Pick-up (Pipe effect)—Cue 1c.
On Scream and Slide—Cue 1d.
PREZ *joins " Steam Heat " * BOYS *for call.*
As all four exit D.R.—*Cue 2, Grey Drop away.*
When Kitchen and PREZ *set—Cue 3.*
*If applause long enough, three " Steam Heat " * BOYS *take call—*
Lime on.

ACT II—SCENE 2.   KITCHEN OF BABE'S HOUSE

The setting is the same as in Act I, Scene 8, except that this time there are five chairs around the kitchen table.
JOE *is seated* D.S. *of table,* BRENDA L. *of table,* PREZ *standing* U.S. *of table,* MAE *seated to his* R. BABE *goes to cupboard* U.L., *gets bottle of beer and sits* R. *end of table.* MAE *is drinking from beer bottle. There are beer cans and bottles and mugs on table.*

PREZ.   **Listen, Mae, pay attention to the meeting and quit guzzling all this free beer.**
MAE.   **I ain't guzzling, I'm just being sociable.**
PREZ.   **Well this ain't a sociable, this is an official meeting.**
BABE.   **Mae's got to keep her strength up.**
PREZ.   **We can't just sit around here and do nothing, we got to make plans. Hasler ain't going to give in easy.**
BRENDA.   **We got the slow-down.**

Warn Sound.

PREZ [*To* BRENDA].   **I mean other things, more like for instance, like why a suggestion here from Jake Fondermeyer.** [*Takes letter out of pocket. To others.*] **He says when he was working at the Ironclad Overall Company and they was having trouble, why they spit tobacco juice in the back hip pockets of the overalls.**
MAE [*Rises*].   **I draw the line at chewing tobacco.**
PREZ.   **I wasn't suggesting that.**

MAE sits.

BRENDA. **How about if the packers put the size large bottoms with the size small tops, and like that?**

JOE. **Sure.**

PREZ [*Pointing to* BRENDA]. **Now that's what I mean. That's CONSTRUCTIVE.**

Phone rings.
BABE rises, crosses to phone D.R.

That's clear thinking.

BABE [*To phone*]. **Hello—oh—sure. Sure I recognise your voice.**

MAE [*Continuing the conversation so that they won't seem to be listening*]. **But that wouldn't take effect soon enough,**

BRENDA. **Well I suppose not.**

BABE [*In phone*]. **Yes, I am.**

PREZ [*Crossing far* L.]. **Let's be practical.**

MAE [*Rises*]. **Oh, I'm going to break down and have another beer!** [*Crosses to cupboard* U.L. *and gets beer—crosses back to chair and sits.*]

BABE [*In phone*]. **No, I can't talk now. I've been away three days.**

MAE [*Crosses back to table*]. **We got to put the screws on them right now, not later.** [*Sits.*]

BABE [*In phone*]. **Look, I have several people here. It wouldn't do any good, anyhow. So goodbye, I'm sorry.** [*Hangs up.*]

PREZ [*Steps* C.]. **Babe, they've been saying . . .** [*Turns to others abruptly.*] **Look, I don't want to get Babe into trouble but . . .**

BABE. **Go ahead. What trouble can you get me into? I'm fired already.** [*Sits.*]

MAE. **Well, the union ought to do something about that too.**

PREZ. **If she hadn't stood right up and said she did it, we could have. But if somebody up and admits they been bustin' up the company property . . .** [*Leans into them at table.*] **Listen, here's a confidence just inside the committee. Some of the buttons ain't been sewed on too good. Wait until the salesmen come screaming back to Hasler.**

POP enters C.

POP. **Hello.**

PREZ. **Mr. Williams.**

POP. **Big meeting hey.** [*To* BABE.] **Hi ya, honey.**

BABE. **Hi ya, Pop.**

POP. **Don't let me interrupt.**

BABE. **How was your trip?**

POP. **Dirty—got another hot box. On the siding for twenty-five minutes.** [*Exits door* L.]

PREZ. **Well, that's about it anyhow.** [*Crosses far* L.]

They all rise. MAE *crosses to* PREZ, *who is putting jacket on, which was lying on Morris chair.*   Warn Train Whistle.

MAE. **Sure**

JOE [*Puts coat on from back of chair—Crosses to between* BRENDA *and* BABE, *who are standing* U.S. *of table.*] **And let's all be thinking about new ways to jam things up.**

BRENDA. **Much obliged for the beer.**

BABE. **That's all right.**

MAE. **What do you mean, you can't take me home?**

PREZ. **Listen, Mae, my wife will be raising hell.**

MAE. **Too bad you didn't think of that before.** [*Starts to exit* U.C.]

PREZ [*Grabbing her*]. **Listen, I'll take you home, Mae.**

MAE. **Don't bother.** [*She crosses to door.*]

PREZ. **But Mae, there's prowlers out at this hour of the night.**

MAE. **Single ones, I hope.**

MAE exits, followed by PREZ.

BRENDA. **Come on, Joe.**

JOE *and* BRENDA *exit.* Train Whistle go.
POP enters from L.

POP. **Say, I stopped in down at the corner tavern for a beer just now and guess who I run into.** [*Standing* C.]

BABE [*Crossing to him*]. **Old man Hasler and Rita Hayworth?**

POP. **No, Sid.**

BABE. **Sid!** [*Turns, moves to* U.R. *corner of table.*] **What's he up to?**

POP. **The way I got it, he just been phoning you or something of that kind. What happened between you?**

BABE. **Never mind, Pop.**

POP. **That's what I told Sid. I told him forget it and come on up.**

BABE. Oh, Pop, you're too fresh.

POP. That boy don't feel good about something.

BABE. Neither do I.

There is a knock on the door C.

Music No. 17A. **" SMALL TALK "** *Incidental*

POP [*Opens door, steps* L.]. **Come on in, Sid.**

SID *opens the door and stands there looking at them*

BABE [*With veiled sarcasm*]. **Yes, do come in.**

POP. **Make yourself at home.** [*Crosses* L. *Exits.*]

SID [*Closes door*]. **Have you really been away?**

BABE [*Crosses* L. *to above Morris chair, facing* L.]. **Sure. I went to Chicago to visit the Lincoln Park Zoo.**

SID [*Crosses to her*]. **Just because we're on different sides, is that any reason for you and me to get all balled-up?**

BABE [*Turns to him*]. **Looks like it, doesn't it?**

SID. **Not to me it doesn't.** [*Tries to hug her—she pulls away.*] **What kind of a queen are you anyway?** [*Breaks back irritably from her and moves* D.R. *of Morris chair.*]

BABE [*From behind Morris chair*]. **Haven't you heard? I'm the sweetheart of the Local 343 Associated Garment Workers of North America. My gosh, Sid, I warned you, I told you. You knew all about how I felt.** [*Step far* L.] **I happen to think there are certain things a person has to stand for in this life. But I guess you've forgotten all about that.**

SID. **I forget nothing. They pay me to run the factory.**

BABE. **So run the factory. You stick to your side and I'll stick to mine.** [*Turns, steps* L.]

SID [*Crosses below chair to* D.L.]. **Listen, Miss Williams. I love you. Corny, ain't it?**

Music stops.

Did you hear me?

BABE [*Nods*]. **Yes.**

SID. **Babe, can't you see my side of it? I can't fail at this. I was a cutting foreman when I bluffed my way into this job and I'm going to fight to stay here. And now that I've got you in my plane—** [*He tries to take her in his arms.*] **I'm fighting even harder.**

BABE. **Watch those hands, tycoon.** [*Steps* L.]

POP *enters from* L., *with stamp album.* SID *crosses to table, sits chair* L.   Warn Cues 3a, 4 and 5, Limes and Flys.

POP. **Well, here we are.**

BABE. **What you got there, Pop, your stamp album?**

POP. **Now don't get excited. If Sid doesn't want to look at it, why he don't have to.** [*Crosses to table.*] **No law against my looking at it, is there?** [*Clears space on table, puts album down.*]

BABE. **But Sid likes stamps. He told me so; don't you, Sid?**

SID. **Yeah. I was looking at it the other night.**

POP. **Sure! There's universal appeal in stamps. I knew you'd be interested.**

BABE. **Sid's very interested . . . but me . . . I'm just plain bushed.** [*Starts for door* L.] **You don't mind if I slide off to bed?**

POP. **Run along, honey. Good night, dear.**

SID. **Good night. Sleep well.**

BABE. **Thanks.** [*Hand on door knob—Exits* L.]

Music No. 18. **" HEY THERE "** *Reprise*

POP [*Sits at chair* U.R. *of table. Spoken*]. **Sid, suppose we start with the Pan American ISSUES of 1901.**

Cue 3a.

SID [*Spoken*]. **I guess that's as good a place to start off as any.**

The Kitchen Lights dim down. BABE *appears at bedroom panel.*

Limes go.

BABE, *lit by the lime, steps* D.S.L.

BABE [*Singing—crosses* D.S.].

Hey there! You with the stars in your eyes,
Love never made a fool of you,
You used to be too wise!
Hey there! You on that high flyin' cloud,
Though you've been acting cold to him
You know your heart is sold to him,
Get on the ball, girl,

> Just take it all in your stride,
> Don't let him make you fall apart,
> You've always had your pride.
> Won't you take this advice I hand you like a brother?
> Or are you not seeing things too clear,
> Are you too much in love to hear . . . .

Cue 4.

Breaks down—cries—covers face with R. *hand—(when Lime out exits* D.L.*). Music continues.*

On Orchestra Cue—" —is it all going IN "
—Lime Out.

On Orchestra Cue " —out the OTHER "—Elevator Cloth in.
When Cloth in, and on last chord of music—Cue 5.

ACT II—SCENE 3.   TICK-TOCK SCENE

The setting is the same as in Act I, Scene 9

Music No. 18A.   FACTORY MUSIC

FOUR GIRLS *enter* L., *another* GIRL *enters fast from* R. *three more*
GIRLS *enter* R.

1ST GIRL.   **Hey, Sarah, are you crazy? Slow down.**

2ND GIRL.   **Nobody's looking.**

1ST GIRL.   **Here comes Mr. Hines.**

2ND GIRL.   **Oh, excuse me.** [*Suddenly goes into a slow motion walk, like the other* GIRLS.]

HINES [*Enters* R. *and looks at the* GIRLS *who are all walking slowly. Crosses to* C.].   **I hate women, that's what I do. Especially young flibberty-gibbets.**

GIRLS *toss heads.*

Girls! Girls!

GIRLS *stop walking.*

You are a disgrace to my training.   [C.]   **You are hurting my feelings.**
[*Puts his arm over his eyes.*]

GIRLS *rush to* HINES *in sympathy, and surround him.*
Music fades.

1ST GIRL.   **Oh, Mr. Hines, we didn't mean to hurt your feelings.**

3RD GIRL.   **Oh, I'm sorry.**

2ND GIRL.   **It's nothing personal, Mr. Hines.**

HINES.   **It cuts. It cuts. I have a notion to throw away my stop watch and give up.**

ALL GIRLS.   **Oh, no, please don't do that. Oh, no, Hineszie!**

1ST GIRL.   **We'd let you train us all over again.**

SALESMAN [*Enters* D.L.]   **Where's Mr. Hasler?**

HINES.   **I thought you were in Peoria.**

SALESMAN [*Crossing in front to stage* R.].   **I ask for Mr. Hasler and I get Peoria. Don't tell me you're part of this slowdown. Never mind, I'll find him.**
[*Exits* R.]

HINES.   **Did you hear that?**

4TH GIRL.   **He seemed awfully upset.**

HINES.   **To accuse *ME* of a slowdown—**

2ND GIRL.   **Oh, not you.**

HINES.   **Me, me— a man who has lived his life by the clock.**

2ND GIRL.   **We're sorry, Mr. Hines.**

Music No. 19.   " THINK OF THE TIME I SAVE "

5TH GIRL.   **We'll be good!**

ALL GIRLS [*Nod*].   **Sure!**

HINES [*Sings, strolling from* D.R.].
> **I'm a time study man,**

GIRLS *cross arms and step* R.L. 2nd *position.*

> **And a time study man can't waste time.** [*Shakes head " no ".*]
> **For a time study man to waste time—**
> **Is a crime.**

R.L.R.   GIRLS *turn around—shift weight, start* L. *and* R.   GIRLS *have*
hands behind them.

> **So I'm ruled by the tick tick tock—**
> **And I live my life by the clock!**
> **I live** [*Stops* R.] **my life by the tick tick tock**
> [*Three tiny knee bends.*]
> **Of the clock.**

GIRLS move into position. HINES sits on seat made of two GIRLS'
backsides.

When I go to sleep
I don't undress, [*Lean in on " undress ".*]
Oh yes, I sleep in all my clothes,
I must confess, [*Back.*]
You say a strange way to behave,

GIRLS nod heads " yes '

Well I will admit that the suit gets mussed
And it gathers lint and it picks up dust,
But think of the time I save! [*Hat.*]

GIRLS.   Think [*Fingers.*] of the time he saves!

Music interlude. HINES does step turning to face girls and around
again to audience. GIRLS bob heads. HINES' dance 3-8's x 5.
GIRLS on knees—1-2 GIRLS get on knees—bow heads as he passes.
Shift into knee position again on 5.   *Sits on bed.*

HINES.   The alarm clock rings
4th GIRL [*Spoken*].   Brrrrr—
HINES [*Puts alarm off—pats GIRL's head*].
                It's 6 a.m.
And then right there in bed I shave, [*Lean in.*]
Takes GIRL's arm, uses as razor strop.]
That's what I said, [*Lean out.*]
While I am still in bed I shave [*Nods " yes ".*]
Well, the lather drips and the bed gets wet,
And oh what a lousy [*Gets up.*] shave I get,
But think of the time I save!
[*Hat.*]

GIRLS [*Fingers*].
                Think of the time he saves!   [*On knees.*]

GIRLS up 8 wait toes in. HINES goes back and dances C.

Tick tock, tick tock, tempus fugit,

GIRLS on S.R. use R. shoulder.

Tick tock, tick tock, time goes by.

GIRLS on S.L. use L.. Watch.

HINES.   How I love to sit and watch the seconds multiply!

HINES goes forward. Goes behind GIRLS C. GIRLS take positions.

At breakfast time

Feet apart, GIRLS get into positions. Small steps.

I grab a bowl
And in the bowl I drop an egg,
Then add some juice, [*Leaning.*]
A poor excuse for what I crave, [*Nods " yes "*]
And then I'll add some oatmeal too— [*Pause*].
And it comes out tasting just like glue,
But think of the time I save!   [*Hat.*]

GIRLS [*S.L. use L. finger. S.R. use R. finger. Finger*].
                Think of the time he saves!

                                    Warn Cues 6 and 7, Flys and Limes.
Music Interlude.
GIRLS wait four fast counts or two slow ones. Drop hands sharply
down. Go backwards 4 x 8 in 2nd position alternating foot.
HINES goes back C., and dances.

Tick tock, tick tock, tempus fugit,
Tick tock, tick tock, time goes by.

Small Chaplin-like step L.—up—slide on R.—2 steps—repeat.
Small Chaplin-like step on R.L. lifted faces front—repeat 4 times.
Stop—lean in—S.L. backs to and close together. S.R. front to and
same.

HINES.   I'll keep sitting counting seconds till the day I die,
[*Comes forward.*]
And when I do,

GIRLS—bent over go to formation 4 group—2 at ends.

I have a plan,
Before I'm dead
I'll dig my grave,

TWO END-GIRLS S.R. and S.L.

That's what I said
Before I'm dead I'll dig my grave. [*Lies on grave.*]
'Cuz when St. Peter calls my name,

I know I'll get there just the same,
But think of the time I'll save!
[*Hat.*]

GIRLS.   Think of the time he'll save! [*Up and finger on " think ".*]
Music.
GIRLS *exit* R.—*Chaplin-like step large—face in direction that they go. On* R.—L. *up.* HINES *tags on to last* GIRL—*does spin—raises his hat as the lights go out—exits* D.R.
When Hines raises his hat—Cue 6, Limes out.
When Lights out—Elevator Cloth away.
When Cloth away and Desk set—Cue 7.

ACT II—SCENE 4. THE OFFICE

The setting is the same as in Act I, Scene 4, except that the single chair L. *of desk* R. *is now set in the* U.L. *corner,* L. *of the window* U.L. *The lights come up revealing* MABEL *seated at her desk* L. *reading her newspaper, and* SID *at his desk, on the telephone.* MABEL *facing* D.S. *at desk.*

MABEL [*Reading*].   " Teen Age Girl Confesses."
SID [*In the phone*].   I can't help it. It's the slowdown.
MABEL.   " Teen Age Boy Attacks School Teacher ". Tch, Tch, tch.
SID.   They'll get the pajamas somewhere else if we don't make deliveries. Well, that's not my department. [*Hangs up.*]
MABEL.   " Teen Age Sex Orgies Revealed." Isn't that terrible?
SID.   They sure have more fun nowadays than when I was a kid.
HASLER *enters* R. *Crosses to* C.
MABEL [*Hurriedly putting newspaper away*].   Good morning, Mr. Hasler.
HASLER [*Crosses to* MABEL].   A slowdown like this proves what I've said for years. Nobody is interested in work.
MABEL.   That's right! [*Turns to desk—turns chair in.*]
HASLER.   The whole country is on the skids. Here I am right now with employees openly defiant of top management.
SID [*Rising*].   Look, Mr. Hasler. Maybe if we offered a compromise.
MABEL *picks up papers.*
HASLER [*Steps to desk*].   Not until there's ice in hell three feet thick. [*Hits desk.*] I'm a fighter, Sorokin. [*Assumes John L. Sullivan pose.*]
SID.   We've got hundreds of orders to get out . . .
MABEL [*Rises, gets a letter, crosses to* HASLER C.].   That's right, Mr. Hasler. Here's a letter from Marx and Klein over to Fort Wayne, Indiana . . .
HASLER [*Crossing* L. *in front of* MABEL].   Marx and Klein? Damn chain outfit. Damned Communists! Want another price cut I suppose.
MABEL [*Crossing to him*].   Well, they say unless we take care of this shipment—
HASLER.   Now, Mabel, don't stand there and try to tell me about Marx and Klein—I've been dealing with them for twenty years. [*Crosses* D.L.]
MABEL.   But, Mr. Hasler, they say . . . [*Sits.*]
Enter SALESMAN R.
SALESMAN [*Crosses to* C.].   I've been looking for you, Mr. Hasler.
HASLER.   Why aren't you out on the territory? What are you doing here?
SALESMAN.   Because of what happened in Peoria.
HINES [*Enters* R., *distracted, crosses to between* SID *and* SALESMAN].   The elevator's stuck.
SALESMAN.   Hey! You, Hines, what size are you?
HINES.   Size? Me? What is this? The elevator is stuck.
SALESMAN.   You look like a medium. I need you.
SALESMAN *crosses to desk, opens box.*
HASLER.   What on earth is going on around here?
SALESMAN [*At desk, opens box and takes out pajama trousers*].   Take your pants off.
HINES [*From* C. *to* SALESMAN].   I'll do no such thing.
SALESMAN.   Mr. Hasler, this is life and death to the Sleep Tite organisation. I want him to model these pajamas.
SALESMAN *holds up pajama trousers.*
HASLER [*Crosses to* L. *of* HINES].   Hines, take your pants off.
HINES.   Okay, chief. [*Starts to take off pants.*] Me, honest? [*Pulls them on again.*]
SALESMAN.   Come on, come on.
MABEL.   Oh what a day. [*Covers her face with her hands.*]
HINES.   I'm a very busy man. I'm a Time Study man, not a model.
SALESMAN.   This is all for Sleep Tite, Mister.
HASLER.   Hines . . . put those pajamas on.
HINES.   Okay, Chief.

HINES takes off his trousers, puts them on chair U.L., *puts on pajama pants. As he is putting them on* HASLER *speaks.*

HASLER.   **Hurry it up.** [*Crosses* D.L.] **Let's get it over with, whatever it is.**

SALESMAN.   **Now, Mr. Hasler, I want you to get the picture.   I was showing this to Charley Robertson of Robertson Brothers.   Now I ain't one of your type salesman that believe in half-measures.   Whenever I have a sample room I do just what we got Hineszie doing.   I model the pants myself.**

By this time HINES *is awkwardly modelling the pajamas. He strikes various poses—lies on the floor different ways—when he curls up* HASLER *speaks.*

HASLER.   **Beautiful styling.   What more do you want?**

HINES rises, stands with hands behind back and (unseen by audience) undoes the catch at the back of the pajama pants.

SALESMAN.   **Now wait . . . Here I am in Peoria and I'm modelling the pants.   Mr. Robertson and his two buyers are very impressed with the line and ready to buy.   Get the picture?**

HASLER.   **Go on, go on.   I hope there's some point to all this.**

SALESMAN [*Pointing at* HINES].   **Hines, now take a deep breath, stick out your stomach.**

HINES.   **This is truly ridiculous.**

SALESMAN.   **Everybody bear in mind I got these pajamas out of stock, right out of the box.**   [*Pounding box.*]   **Go on Hines, breathe in.**

HASLER.   **He said to breathe.   Breathe.   Let's get it over.**

HINES takes a powerful breath. The button pops off the pants and down they go.

My God!

HINES.   **Oh, I'm sorry.** [*Starts to recover the pants.*]

SALESMAN.   **No, leave 'em lay.**

HINES straightens up. GLADYS *enters* U.L., *carrying ledger—sees* HINES—*screams and turns to* MABEL *for protection.*

GLADYS.   **What are you doing, Vernon?   Playing games?**

MABEL [*Rising, turns to* GLADYS].   **Mr. Hines.   Really.** [*Puts arm around* GLADYS *and turns her away.*]

SID.   **Let me see those.** [*Crosses to* HINES—*gets pajamas and returns to* D.R. *corner of desk.*]

SALESMAN.   **They're all like that.   Every one.   Boxes and boxes of them.**

HASLER.   **What's the idea?   Who did this?**

SID [*At desk*].   **Somebody's got quite a sense of humour.**

HASLER [*Crosses to desk*].   **What the hell are you talking about?**

SID.   **Two threads in every waistband button.**

HASLER.   **What?**

SID.   **They're not sewed on.   Only two threads.** [*Crosses* U.S. *of desk and picks up phone.*]   **Somebody's being very cute.**

HASLER.   **Cute!   Sabotage!   Open rebellion!**

HINES [*Crosses to* HASLER].   **On the other hand, it might be just coincidence.**

HASLER.   **Oh, put your pants on.** [*Turns* U.S. *and examines pajamas.*]

HINES crosses U.S. *to pants, which* GLADYS *hands him back to front.*

GLADYS [*Aside to him*].   **What did you do, Vernon?**

HINES [*Taking pants without looking at them*].   **I didn't do anything.**

SID [*In the phone*].   **Gimme the stock-room.**

SALESMAN [*Crosses to* MABEL *and turns*].   **I'll be the laughing stock of the pajama game.**

HINES puts pants on backwards—zips where there is no zipper— GLADYS *tries to help. He pushes her off.* HINES *turns back on audience—puts pants on correctly.*

MABEL [*To* SALESMAN].   **You never finished your story.   What did this Robertson do when your pants fell down?**

SALESMAN.   **He laughed.   No sense of humour.**

HINES [*To* GLADYS, *who is trying to help him—in the laughter of the audience*].   **Keep your hands off me.**

SID [*In phone*].   **Hold the orders till we've checked the stock.   I'll be right down.** [*To* SALESMAN.]   **Come on, Max.**

HINES is having trouble with zipper—still has back to audience as he tugs at it. SID *exits* R., *followed by* SALESMAN.

HASLER [*Crosses to* MABEL].   **If they think they can lick Myron Hasler with this sort of trickery they got another guess coming.   I'm a fighter.   Damn Communists.** [*Turns to* HINES.]   **Hines!   Get dressed, you idiot.   I want a time report on each individual worker.**

HINES *redoubles his efforts to fix his zipper while* HASLER *keeps shouting at him. Eventually* HINES *turns to* HASLER *in despair, holds his* L. *arm up and the audience sees that his shirt cuff is caught in the zipper—*HASLER *fumes—*HINES *crosses* R. *helplessly— gets tangled up in hat-rack—then exits* R. HASLER *follows him still shouting, then sits at* R. *desk.*

MABEL [*Gets letter, crosses to* HASLER]. **Now, Mr. Hasler, in this letter from Marx and Klein, they say . . .**

HASLER. **Don't bother me with letters from Marx and Klein or anybody else.**

MABEL. **Well . . .**

HASLER. **Especially Marx and Klein, those damn pirates.**

MABEL *shrugs, crosses back to desk* L. *and sits.*

[*To* GLADYS.] **Gladys, don't forget I've got a meeting of the Board of Directors tomorrow.** [*Puts head in hands.*]

GLADYS [*Crosses to his* L.]. **Yes, sir. The books are all ready except—**

HASLER. **Two threads. That's what I got to tell them. Two threads.**

SID *enters* R. *Crosses to front of desk* R.

SID. **We've got to recall an awful lot of orders.**

HASLER. **How many?**

SID [*Crossing* L. *to* MABEL]. **They're gonna let us know.**

HASLER. **Gladys, give me your entry.**

GLADYS *hands him ledger which he peruses.*

SID. **Clear out for a while, will you, Mabel?**

MABEL [*Picking up her belongings, rises and crosses to door* L.]. **Oh sure. I'll get something to settle my stomach.**

MABEL *exits* U.L.

HASLER [*To* GLADYS]. **Have it ready for the meeting tomorrow, that's all.**

GLADYS *exits* R. *with ledger.* HASLER *starts to cross* U.L.

SID. **Mr. Hasler.**

HASLER [*Stopping*]. **Yeah?**

SID. **I'd like to make a pitch.**

HASLER. **Pitch? All right. Pitch ahead.**

SID [*Crosses slowly to* HASLER]. **Before we get started let me make my position clear.** [*Crosses* R. *to below desk* R.] **I'm for the company first, last and always. But labour problems have got to end up in one way . . . compromise.** [*Turns to* HASLER.]

HASLER. **Sorokin . . .** [*Crosses down to* L. *of* SID.] **you've been around here long enough to learn something. But you seem a little slow. I'm a fighter.** [*Adopts John L. Sullivan pose.*] **Keep your dukes up, boy.** [*Crosses to door* U.L.]

SID [*Following him*]. **Yes, but . . .**

HASLER. **Don't waste your breath on me.** [*Adopts fighting stance.*] **Keep your dukes up.**

HASLER *exits* L. *As he is saying his last line,* GLADYS *enters* R.

GLADYS. **Dukes up? What does that mean?**

SID [*Crosses* D.S. *to desk* R.]. **Mr. Hasler wants me to take boxing lessons.**

GLADYS [*Steps* D.S.—*laughing*]. **You certainly are a character.**

SID. **And I'd like to get some information from you too.**

GLADYS. **What kind?**

SID [*Sits on edge of desk*]. **Double entry.**

GLADYS [*Crosses a few steps to* C.]. **Well, you're not going to get any information, so there.**

SID. **Come here. I'm a desperate man and I hate to ask a cute kid like you to do me a favour.**

GLADYS [*Crossing to him, and sits* L. *end of desk*]. **Sid, dear, you wouldn't have me violate a trust, would you?**

SID. **I sure would. If it would help to unsnarl things around here.**

GLADYS. **Why is that so important?**

SID. **Because my future depends upon the titanic struggle for pajama survival.**

GLADYS [*Laughs*]. **You're a scream.**

Warn Cues 8, 9 and 9a, Flys and Traveller.

SID. **And I just feel that if I knew a little more about the bookkeeping of this—**

GLADYS [*Quickly crosses* C. *moving her ledger farther away from him*]. **Oh no, not that.**

SID. **Oh! I wouldn't ask you to show it to me. Just leave it around.**

GLADYS. **No. Besides it's locked anyhow.**

SID. **I know a sexy dame who'd lend me the key.**

GLADYS [*Crossing to* L. *of* SID *sits on desk edge*]. **Oh, you think so?**

SID. **Well, it would be fun trying to persuade her.**

GLADYS. Well, it might be fun to be persuaded—only you'd be sore when you
   didn't get it.
SID. Oh no, Gladys, I'm grown up.
GLADYS. Quit kidding me. [*Leans in as if to kiss him—then gets up suddenly
   and runs* U.L.] Well, I got to go.
SID [*Stopping her*]. No, wait.
GLADYS [*Turns challengingly*]. What?
SID [*Rises, crosses* C.]. Let's go out tonight.
GLADYS. Well, I hope you're not serious about that key.
SID. I don't feel like being serious about anything. You're busy, huh?
GLADYS [*Crosses* D.R., *and putting the ledger on* R. *desk as she passes it*]. No, and I sure
   would like to, but—oh, gee. Where will you take me?
SID. Any place you say.
GLADYS. I know a wonderful JOINT.

Cue 8.
GLADYS *is* D.S.C.—*she looks* R. *and* L., *then motions to* SID *to join
her.*
As SID *moves* D.S.—Close Traveller.
When Traveller is half closed—Black Drop in.
When Traveller nearly closed—Cue 9.

Music No. 20. " HERNANDO'S HIDEAWAY "

GLADYS [*Sings*].

I know a dark secluded place, [*Front* C., *gives* R. *hand.*]
A place where no-one knows your face. [L. *hand. Embrace.*]
A glass of wine, [*Looks out—squints.*]
A fast embrace, [*Embraces* SID.]
It's called Hernando's Hideaway! O-lay!!
[*Takes Spanish arm position, then recovers. Crosses with* SID *to* C.]
All you see are silhouettes, [L. *hand out—pulls her with* R.]
And all you hear are castanets, [*Throws her arms high.*]
And no one cares how late it gets, [SID *embraces her.*]
Not at Hernando's Hideaway! O-lay!!

GLADYS *and* SID *dance down* L.
At the Golden Fingerbowl or any place you go, [*Dance* L.]
You will meet your Uncle Max and ev'ryone you know,

SID *goes backwards—then* GLADYS *follows facing him.*
Cue 9a.
Traveller opens.

But if you are sitting close and makin' love to me,
You may take my heart,
You may take my soul,
But not my key!

As GLADYS *and* SID *walk off* L., *the Traveller opens slowly in time
to their walk, and the lights change, revealing the Black Drop.*
Just knock three times and whisper low,— [*Walks* L.]
Leads her off S.L.
That you and I were sent by Joe,
Then strike a match and you will know,
You're in Hernando's Hideaway! Olay!!

SID *reaches for her key—*GLADYS *puts it down her dress and pushes
him off* L. *They exit* L.

Music No. 20A. "HERNANDO'S HIDEWAY" *Dance*

GIRL *and* BOY *enter* R., *and cross to* L. *and exit. They are followed
by* " Steam Heat " BOY *in opera hat and cloak, with* 2ND HELPER
as dwarf with bell coat, with " Hernando's Hideaway " *on back.
They cross to* R.C. *Two* DRUNKS *enter* R. *and cross to* C., *gaze at
two* BOYS. *Three couples enter* R., *and stay* D.R., *gazing at the two*
BOYS. " Steam Heat " BOY *does a Spanish dance, uncovers sign
on back of coat.* " Steam-Heat " BOY *leads them all off,* 2ND
HELPER *last,* D.L. *Three* BOYS *knock on* D.L. *portal.*
When " Steam Heat " BOY *does Spanish Dance*—Warn Cues 10
and 11, Limes and Flys.

THREE BOYS [*Heads round portal.*] Joe sent us!!

The three BOYS *disappear* D.L., *as the stage lights black out, and the
sign lighting for* " Hernando's Hideaway " *is revealed.
Music continues.*
" *Joe sent US* "—Cue 10, Limes out.
On Music change—Cue 11.
When Sign lettering is out—Black Drop away.

ACT II—SCENE 5. HERNANDO'S HIDEAWAY

The scene is in complete darkness. GLADYS *and* SID *are seated* L.
and R. *of a small table* C. *Branching from them to* U.L. *and* U.R.
*is a row of curtained booths. Above the booths is a trellis with
Chinese lanterns suspended in it. Through the windows of the back
wall are the reverse sides of neon beer signs.* D.L. *is a large juke box.*
D.R. *is a small table with three chairs around it.* U.S. *of this table
is a draught screen.*
All this is revealed when the lights come on.
The BOYS *and* GIRLS *move about stage in the darkness during the
number, lighting matches when they have a line to sing.*

(*Music No. 20A—continued.*)

1ST GIRL [*Spoken*]. **Ooh—** [*Laugh—slap.*] **—fresh!**
1ST BOY. **Who's that?**
2ND BOY [*Match*]. **Poopsie—Poopsie—POOPSIE!** [*Into booth* L. *Match out
   before last "Poopsie".*]
3RD BOY [*In booth*]. **Hey, buddie, dis ain't Poopsie!**
POOPSIE [*Sings.* L. *to* C. *Match*].
   I know a dark secluded place.
1ST GIRL [*Sings.* R. *tc* C. *Match*].
   A place where no one knows your face.
2ND GIRL [*Sings.* R. *to* C. *Match*].
   A glass of wine, a fast embrace,
ALL THREE GIRLS.
   It's called Hernando's Hideaway—Olay! [*All three blow out matches
   and return to positions.*]

Three knocks.   Warn Cue 12 and 13.

THREE GIRLS AND BOY [*Spoken*]. **Joe sent us!**
ALL. **Sssssh!**
2ND BOY [*Match*]. **Poopsie, Poopsie.** [*Crosses* L. *to* R.—*Match out.*]
1ST GIRL [*Sings* R.C. *Match*].
   At the Golden Fingerbowl or any place you go.

*Music—*1ST BOY *slides forward on stomach with match.*

1ST BOY [*Sings* L.C. *Match*].
   You will meet your Uncle Max and everyone you know,

*Music—*3RD BOY—*match on top of juke box.*

2ND BOY [*Sings.* L.C. *Match*].
   But if you go to the spot that I am thinking of,
POOPSIE [*Match*].
   You will be free,
1ST BOY [*Match*].
   To gaze at me,
ALL.   **And talk of LOVE.**

ALL *light matches on "love*
ALL *matches light.*
ALL *come forward slowly in long line across front.*

[*Sing sotto voce.*]
   Just knock three times and whisper low,
   That you and I were sent by Joe,
   Then strike a match and you will know

Cue 12.
ALL *blow matches out—lights.*

   You're in Hernando's Hideaway
   [*Lean on* L. *foot front,* L., *hand at mouth.*]
   OLAY!

Slow movement with L. *arm* L.
Music—Boom—All in Spanish poses.
*Music—*ALL *run into booths.*   Cue 13.
*All lights are now on, and the audience sees the scene as described
at the opening.*

GLADYS [*Seated* L. *at table* C.]. **I want to ask you a personal question, Sid. Do
   you like Scotch?**
SID [*Seated* R. *at table* C.]. **No, Gladys, I don't like Scotch.**
GLADYS. **Neither do I. Scotch has a very peculiar taste.**

WAITER *enters. from* L. *with tray, crosses to table* C., *puts glass on
table.*

SID. **Kind of Scotch-like taste?**
GLADYS. **Yeah, that's it, count me out.** [*To waiter.*] **Is that gin?**
WAITER. **Yes, ma'am.**
GLADYS [*Tastes it—makes an ugly face*]. **You're right.**

41

GUESTS step D.R., from booths and table and mill around. WAITER exits R.

You know I can't figure you out, Sid. I guess when you first came here, you caught on that I thought you were cute, but you never gave me a tumble till tonight.

SID. I told you what I was up to, didn't I?

GLADYS. I forget. Tell me again.

SID. I'm gonna get you fried and get that key away from you.

GLADYS [*Singing—to far end of room*]. You'll never get my key. You'll never get my key.

Juke box starts to play.

Music No. 20B. " HERNANDO'S HIDEAWAY " *Incidental*

SID. Shhh. They'll hear you.

GLADYS. You think I'm terrible, don't you?

BABE and PREZ enter D.R. and cross to group sitting at table D.R.

1ST GIRL [*Rising*]. Hey! I thought you were at the bowling alley.

PREZ. We was.

1ST GIRL. Who won?

PREZ. Babe wanted to come here.

BABE. I gotta give a message to somebody.

People block her vision—and she doesn't see SID.

PREZ. We was gonna get thrown out anyways. Hineszie came in drunk and started raising a ruckus.

2ND GIRL. Did you bowl good, Babe?

BABE. No, this wasn't my night.

GLADYS. Come on, let's dance. [*Rises—crosses to R. of SID and holds her arms up.*]

SID. Okay. [*Rises—turns to dance with GLADYS—sees BABE—turns and sits down again.*]

2ND GIRL. Babe, you're coming to the Union Rally, aren't you?

BABE. Well, sure—what do you think?

GLADYS. What's the matter Sid?

SID. I don't feel so good.

GLADYS. You sick, you mean?

SID. Not sick—just kind of depressed.

GLADYS. Oh look—don't be depressed. [*Takes key from around her neck.*] Wait a minute—look what I'm giving you. There it is—See? [*Crosses L.—sits.*] Take it.

SID. This is a lousy trick, Gladys.

GLADYS. I'll lend it to you. But don't tell anybody, and you gotta give it back in the morning.

SID. Thanks a helluva lot.

GLADYS. Now you gonna cheer up?

BABE crosses to table C. Stays D.R. of SID. PREZ sits R. of table D.R. with 2ND GIRL on his knee.

Hi, Babe.

SID [*Rises*]. Yes, hello.

GLADYS. Sid and I are just old friends.

SID. Won't you join us?

BABE. No, thank you. Gladys, I just come in to tell you that Hineszie's out for blood!

GLADYS. Oh, Hineszie!

BABE. He came over to the bowling alley looking for you. He knows you're out with Sid and he's got a knife.

SID. The damn fool.

GLADYS. He's always got a knife. He's living in the past, That's not healthy, do you think so, Sid?

BABE. Look, I didn't come here to be funny, and I didn't come here because I'm craving your company or wanting to join your party or anything like that. I came here to tell you he's dangerous.

GLADYS. He talks dangerous, but he isn't. I think I'll take a nap. [*Bangs her head on the table.*]

BABE turns, crosses to exit R.

SID. Babe, please.

SID tries to stop BABE—steps R. then back C. to GLADYS. BABE exits D.R., followed by 2ND GIRL.

GLADYS. Oh dear, a fallen woman—that's what I am—I lost my key.

SID. I'm gonna get Prez to take you home. Is that all right?

GLADYS. If Mr. Hasler ever finds out.

SID. **He won't find out.**

GLADYS. **I can't face myself. I better take another nap.** [*Bangs head on table again.*]

SID [*Crosses to* PREZ—*takes money out of his pocket*]. **Prez, pay up for me and take Gladys home, will ya?**

PREZ [*Crossing* L. *to table, taking money from* SID]. **Gladys? Oh, sure, sure, Sid. Glad to.**

SID. **I've got some important book-keeping to do.** [*Exits* D.R.]

PREZ [*Crosses to table* C.] **Her is the cutest one.**

GLADYS. **I remember you.** [*Banging head on table again.*]

PREZ. **You got class, you know it?** [*Sits.*] **Her is the cutest.**

MAE [*Pops up from booth* L.C.—*sticks head through lattice work*]. **No, him is the cutest.**

Warn Cues 14 and 15, Flys.

PREZ *rises and backs away to* R.C. MAE *comes out of booth* L. *Crosses to him.*

You cornfed Romeo! I know what goes with you all right, all right. [*Starts after* PREZ, *who crosses* R.] **You snake in the grass. It doesn't matter to you if you break a person's heart. I'll claw your eyes out, I will.** [*Chases him out* R.]

GLADYS. **Encore, encore.** [*Puts head back on table.*]

HINES *enters from* U.L., *drunk, crosses to* L. *of* GLADYS—*stamps foot three times—drops knife, while she is watching him.*

Oh, I see you. You don't need to drop anything.

HINES. **You abandoned woman—you hussy.** [*Picking up knife.*]

GLADYS [*Rises*]. **After the way you behaved.**

WAITER *strikes table* R. *chair and two glasses—exits* R.

Taking your pants off in Mr. Hasler's office.

HINES *puts his arm around her shoulders. She pushes him away.*

GLADYS. **Don't touch me! Prez will see me home.** [*Crosses to* R.—*staggering.*] **And I'm glad I never married you!** [*Exits* D.R.]

Music No. 21 and No. 21A. **" I'LL NEVER BE JEALOUS AGAIN "** *Ballet*

HINES [*Spoken*]. **Prez, Sid, Tom, Dick, Harry—** [*Staggers* D.C.-*crosses back* U. *to chair* C., *falls into it.*] **I CAN see what marriage with Gladys would be like.**

Cue 14.

When stage lights out—Lantern Cloth away.

When Hideaway 6 ft. open—Cue 15.

When the stage lights go out, the lantern cloth flies away—the booths of Hernando's Hideaway swivel open revealing the " Jealousy " Ballet set. Property men strike the juke box D.L. *in the darkness. Five girls strike the table, three chairs and the screen* D.R., *in the darkness.*

ACT II—SCENE 5A. "JEALOUSY" BALLET

Ballet, depicting HINES' *jealousy. Against the* R. *wall is a low double bed which is covered by a lace cover on top of a purple bed-spread. On the bed are two lace-covered bolsters, a large French doll, numerous small lace-covered cushions, and a perfume-atomiser. There is a narrow door set* C. *in the back wall. Above this door is a large moose head, whose eyes light up red during the ballet.*

On the wall L. *is a large wardrobe in the back of which is an exit for* HINES *to go through during the ballet.*

HINES *sits brooding on chair* C. GLADYS *enters* D.R., *dressed in a sleazy bathrobe, with curlers in her hair. She is a terrible sight.*

Warn moose-eye effect.

GLADYS *scrubs floor* L. *of* HINES—*He indicates to her that she must close up the top of her robe. She does so, and starts to rise from the floor.*

As GLADYS *rises from the floor.*—Eyes go.

This is a signal to her that a man is coming, so she dashes round getting HINES *off to work.* HINES *pantomimes husband going off to work and exits* U.C.

After he exits, she is galvanised into action. She takes off her robe, curlers and slippers, puts on high-heeled shoes and a glamorous negligee, picks up atomiser and sprays herself. She then rushes to bed to spray it.

As GLADYS *sprays bed*—Eyes go.

GLADYS *throws spray on bed—sits* L. *end of it.*

HINES *enters* U.C. *as a debonair Frenchman. They make foolish 'ove—dance around—have a pillow fight—dance around again—* GLADYS *dives on bed and Frenchman goes to dive on her.*

When Frenchman goes to dive on GLADYS—Eyes go.

GLADYS *grabs Frenchman and stuffs him into the wardrobe. She picks up the atomiser again and sprays herself. On cue, one of the* BOYS—*dressed exactly like* HINES *as Frenchman rushes out of wardrobe and hits her on head with cushion—rushes back into wardrobe*

GLADYS *lies down on bed prepared for next visitor.*

HINES *enters* U.C. *again. This time as* WRESTLER. *(Kind of Gorgeous George.) They wrestle on bed, then wrestle stage* C.

GLADYS *escapes from his grip—he looks for her—she kisses him on* R. *cheek.*

When GLADYS *kisses Wrestler—Eyes go.*

GLADYS *stuffs Wrestler into wardrobe.*

Warn Cue 20, Flys.

GLADYS *takes off her negligee—puts on her frumpy bathrobe and curlers—starts scrubbing floor again.*

HINES *enters* U.C. *as her husband again—crosses down to her—sniffs the air suspiciously—goes to wardrobe to put his hat and briefcase away.*

As HINES *gets to wardrobe, Frenchman steps out—takes hat and case from* HINES—*they bow to each other—Frenchman re-enters wardrobe.* HINES *crosses* D.S.—*does double-take—rushes back to wardrobe and hammers on door. The door bursts open and* MEN *come plummeting out—surround* HINES *and* GLADYS—HINES *exits* U.C.

Some of the MEN *pick up* GLADYS *and carry her* D.S. *as the lights change and the Black Drop comes in. The rest of the* MEN *stay* U.S. *of the Black Drop.*

On the 18th Count of Music for MEN *out of Wardrobe*—Cue 20, Black Drop in.

GLADYS *does strip in front of drop.*

Warn Cues 21 and 22, Limes and Flys.

HINES *enters* D.R. *and sees* GLADYS—MABEL *(dressed as angel) enters* D.R.—*circles round* HINES, *pacifying him.* HINES *sings " I would trust her—I would trust her "—breaks down and cries on* MABEL'S *shoulders.*

BOYS *carry* GLADYS *off* D.L.—HINES *chases after them with over-sized knife.* MABEL *runs after* HINES. ALL *exit* D.L.

As MABEL *reaches portal leg*—Limes Out, Cue 21.

When lights out—Black Drop away.

When Black Drop away—Cue 22.

ACT II—SCENE 6   THE OFFICE

The setting is the same as for Act I, Scene 4, except that the desk R. *is littered with empty cartons and cups.*

SID *is sitting at desk* R. *with the opened ledger in front of him.*

CHARLIE *enters* R.

CHARLIE. **Sid.** [*Carrying small pair of steps.*]

SID. **'Morning, Charlie.**

CHARLIE [*Crosses to behind* SID]. **There's a committee from the union downstairs waiting to see you.**

SID. **Yeah, I sent for them.**

CHARLIE [*Step to* L. *of him—looks over his shoulder*]. **You been here all night?** [*Crosses to door* L.]

SID. **That's no joke, Charlie, I have.** [*Picks up telephone.*] **I'd like to speak to Mr. Hasler, please.** [*To* CHARLIE.] **And what's more I think I've got something.**

CHARLIE. **Take it easy, boy.** [*He exits* L.]

SID [*In phone*]. **Mr. Hasler, could you come down to the office right away.**

Knock on door R.

Come in. [*In phone.*] **It's pretty important. Thanks.**

Door R. *opens and* PREZ, JOE *and* BABE *enter.*

SID. **Come on in please.**

PREZ *steps to desk,* BABE D.S. *of him,* JOE U.S. *of him.* SID *rises and closes ledger.*

Sorry to have to drag you out so early but I knew you were having a union rally and I wanted to talk to you first.

PREZ. **That's okay, Sid.**

SID. **I think I've got hold of some facts that may clean up this mess.**

PREZ. **Well, it better be quick. Either we get the seven-and-a-half cents or we strike.**

JOE. **You're damned right.**

SID [*Cross to* D.S.L. *corner of desk*].   **What I want to ask is, will you keep your rally going till I get there and talk to you?**

PREZ.   **What about?**

SID.   **About solving this damned thing.**

BABE.   **There ought to be a time limit.**

SID.   **All right, You're going to have a parade?**

JOE.   **We sure are.**

SID.   **That'll give me time. I'll be at the rally.**

PREZ.   **That's fair enough.**

They start out.

SID.   **Oh, Miss Williams, can I speak to you?**

PREZ.   **We'll wait for you downstairs, Babe.**

Motions JOE out of door R.—follows. BABE crosses down to R. of
SID, who is standing at D.L. corner of desk.

Music No. 22.   **" HEY THERE "**   Incidental

SID.   **I know explanations are lousy.**

Warn Cue 23 and Knife effect.

BABE [*Starting to go*].   **Oh, no, Sid, I . . .**

SID [*Grabs her, puts her in chair* L. *of desk*].   **Babe, please!**

BABE.   **Don't.**

SID.   **You've got to let me explain.**

BABE [*Rises, crosses* D.R.].   **I don't want an explanation. It's humiliating.**

SID.   **But you mustn't think . . .**

BABE.   **I don't think anything. I don't care. If you're talking about you and Gladys it's none of my business.**

SID.   **But it *IS* your business.**

BABE [*Crosses* D.L.].   **Oh the hell with that. I'm talking about something bigger.**

SID [*Turns, steps* D.C.].   **Well, this is just great. Can't we even talk to each other and make sense any more?**

BABE.   **I don't see how. Not until this is over.**

SID.   **I've been eating mud long enough. I've had it.**

BABE [*Turns to him*].   **What do you suggest, Sid?**

SID.   **Meet me after the rally.**

BABE.   **I can't, I have a date.** [*Crosses to door* R.]

SID.   **Well, that's that.**

BABE [*At door—turns to him*].   **I'll break it.**

Cue 23.
BABE exits R. SID starts after her. GLADYS screams off L. and
rushes on stopping him. Music fades.

GLADYS.   **Sid, I got to warn you.** [*Grabbing him* U.C.]   **Vernon's not fooling this time. We've been at it all night. We've been screaming and yelling.**

SID.   **Just calm yourself, Gladys. I'll fix everything. I'll take him aside and tell him the whole story.**

HINES appears in doorway R., aims knife, then disappears—unseen
by GLADYS and SID.

In the meantime, here's your key.

SID takes key from pocket and puts it around her neck.

GLADYS.   **Listen—I thought I heard something—**

Clunk. A knife dives into the wall D.S., of L. door. GLADYS
screams and kneels D.S. of chair at desk L. SID stays U.C.

SID [*Yelling*].   **You maniac! You fool!** [*Rushes to door* R.]   **Hineszie, you damn fool!** [*Turns to* GLADYS, *crosses back to* U.C.]

GLADYS.   **I told you I heard something.**

SID [*Crosses back to* GLADYS].   **You heard something all right. Well, I'm glad he's got that out of his system.**

GLADYS.   **How do we know that he has? How do we know.** [*Rising.*]

SID [*Goes to her*].   **Now, Gladys, cut it out.** [*Takes her by shoulders.*]   **It's going to be all right.**

Clunk. Another knife appears in the wall above desk L. GLADYS
screams. SID jumps.

GLADYS.   **You've got to stop him.** [*Kneels down below desk* L.]

SID [*Crosses* U.C.].   **I'll fix that baby . . .**

Picks up window opener for a club and stalks toward door R.
HASLER enters L., fastening his cuffs as though finishing dressing.

HASLER [*Crosses to* U.L.C.].   **I hope this call turns out to be important—**

HASLER is arrested by SID's attitude with club.

What's going on here? [*Sees knife in wall* L.]   **Look! Look! Now, that's not nice. I don't like this. This is company property, Sorokin.**

SID [*Crosses back* C.].   **I'd better explain, Mr. Hasler.**

HASLER. **I think somebody better—**

HASLER. **What the hel.**

    They're trying to murder me.

Clunk. Another knife appears in wall D.S. *of door* L. GLADYS *screams.*

GLADYS *jumps half behind the file cabinet—crouches low.* SID *crosses back* C., *back to wall.* HASLER *ducks down behind chair at desk* L.

Warn off-stage singers.

SID [*Exits* R.]. **I'll stop that.** [*Dashes out after* HINES.]

HASLER [*Hiding behind chair*]. **Call the sheriff.**

GLADYS [*Hiding*]. **You want the sheriff, Mr. Hasler?**

HASLER. **It's a plot to murder me. They've imported gangsters from Chicago. The old Al Capone gang.**

GLADYS. **I don't think so, Mr. Hasler.**

HASLER. **Don't argue with me. Didn't you see those knives? That's the work of FOREIGNERS.**

Chorus O.S.R. *sing "Seven-and-a-half-Cents". Refrain of (music of No. 23)* 1½ *choruses—Fade out.*

GLADYS. **But, Mr. Hasler.**

HASLER. **It's Chicago gangsters.**

GLADYS. **Mr. Hasler, it's—**

HASLER. **They're marching. What's that?** [*Crosses to* L. *window.*]

GLADYS. **No, it's the Union Rally. They're going to have a parade.**

SID *enters* R. *leading* HINES *by the* R. *arm.* HINES *has a bruise on his forehead.* GLADYS *stands up.* SID *pushes* HINES *to* L.C.

HASLER. **Hines, where have you been? On the job, man. The place is full of gangsters. They're out to get me.**

SID. **They're not after YOU, Mr. Hasler. They're after ME.**

HASLER [*Crosses to* SID'S *desk*]. **Talk, talk. Why doesn't somebody do something?** [*Grabs the telephone. In phone.*] **Get me the police.**

SID [*Crosses to* R. *of* HASLER. *Taking the phone away from him and hanging up*]. **You don't want to arrest Hines, do you?**

HASLER. **Hines?**

SID. **He was trying to kill ME.**

HASLER. **He was?** [*Turns to* HINES.] **Hines, suppose you'd succeeded, and me right in the middle of labour troubles. Suppose you'd hit him.**

HINES. **I could have hit him if I'd wanted to. I was just trying to scare him.** [*Hangs his head in shame.*]

HASLER [*Crosses to* SID. *To* SID]. **Is this what you called me about, to come here and endanger my life?**

SID. **No!**

HASLER. **I don't want to be involved in these personal matters.**

SID. **I called you because there's going to be a strike this morning unless you listen to me.**

HASLER. **I told you that I'm a fighter.** [*Adopts stance.*]

SID. **So am I.**

HASLER. **What?**

SID. **Gladys, have his head patched up.** [*Pointing to* HINES.]

GLADYS [*Crosses to* HINES, *takes his* L. *arm. Holds* L. *door open*]. **Come on, Vernon.**

HINES [*Pulling away*]. **Take your hands off me—I'm a fighter.** [*Adopts fighting stance, facing* HASLER.]

GLADYS. **Come on, tiger!**

GLADYS *yanks* HINES *off* L.

Warn Cues 24 and 25, Limes, Flys and Traveller.

SID. **Mr. Hasler, I'm going before the Board of Directors.**

HASLER. **You are WHAT?**

SID. **If I can't solve this any other way.**

HASLER. **Solve what? Sometimes I think—**

SID. **I've been up all night with your ledger.** [*Picks up ledger.*]

HASLER. **What did you say?**

SID. **I apologise. I know you didn't hire me as a safe-cracker, but I had to get some facts. I've been through your books.**

HASLER. **You mean to say that you—**

SID [*Crosses to* HASLER]. **That seven-and-a-half cents was added to the costs six months ago.** [*Turns back to desk.*]

HASLER. **I can put you in jail, that's what I can do. Put you in jail.**

SID. **No you can't.** [*Puts down book.*] **But you can give that raise. If you don't**

I'll go before the Board and tell them the situation, and tell them how many orders have been cancelled.

HASLER.   Not one damn order—

SID.   Read your mail. There's a dozen cancellations. Mabel's tried all day yesterday to tell you about Marx and Klein.

HASLER reacts, takes a step D.S.

And if this operation folds up I fold up with it. And I don't want to. So do me a favour. [*Pushes chair under* HASLER.] **Sit down and talk to me.**

HASLER sits.

(Music Cue—No. 23)

" —and talk to ME "—Cue 24, Limes out.
When lights out—Close Traveller F. Black Drop in.
When Traveller closed—Cue 25.

ACT II—SCENE 7.   SEVEN-AND-A-HALF CENTS AND FINALE

The first part of the scene takes place in front of the Switch Traveller.
When the lights come on BRENDA is seen talking to a group of the
WORKERS D.L.

Music No. 23.   " SEVEN-AND-A-HALF CENTS "   (Under dialogue)

BRENDA [*Talking to group* L.C.]   **Sure, Hasler was in Sorokin's office when we marched by the factory. Now he'll know we mean business.**

1ST GIRL.   **Here comes Prez.**

PREZ enters D.R., wearing a sash, and crosses to L.C.

BRENDA.   **Hey, why ain't you in the parade, Prez?**

MAE enters D.R. and crosses to C.

PREZ.   **I don't want to get out of breath before making my speech.**

2ND GIRL.   **This will wake them up.**

PREZ [*To* MAE].   **Is my ribbon straight?**

MAE.   **I don't know, Why don't you ask your wife.**

BRENDA.   **We're sure to win, ain't we, Prez?**

PREZ.   **What kind of a question is that? Sure we are.**

Babe will tell you.

BABE and POOPSIE enter D.R., followed by more WORKERS.

BABE.   **The answer is yes—that's the answer to everything today. What is it?**

BRENDA.   **I just asked, were we going to win the strike?**

BABE.   **Sure we're going to win, and that ain't all.**

PREZ.   **Babe and me was up half the night figuring things out. I got it all written down on paper.**

BRENDA.   **What do you mean, Prez?**

PREZ.   **Well listen here and I'll tell you.**

[*Sings.*]   **I figured it out,   I figured it out,**
[R.]   [L.]   [BOTH together.]
With a pencil and a pad I figured it out.
[*Waves pencil in* R. *hand, pad in* L.]
Seven-and-a-half cents doesn't buy a helluva lot,
Seven-and-a-half cents doesn't mean a thing, [*Punch.*]
But give it to me every hour, [*Punch.*]
Forty hours every week,
That's enough for me [*Both hands.*] **to be**
Livin' like a king
I figured it out. [*Begins to cross* L. *to* R.]

ALL.   **He figured it out,** [*Hand gestures.*]

PREZ.   **I figured it out,** [*Goes* L. *to* R.]

ALL.   **He figured it out.** [*Same.*]

PREZ.   **With a pencil and a pad** [*Waves pencil in* R. *hand, pad in* L.]
I figured it out. [*Waves both pencil and pad together.*]
Only five years from today;
ALL look at one another.
Only five years from today; [L. *hand point.*]
I can see it all before me, [*Looks front.*]
Only five years from today.

[*Spoken.*]   **" Five years—now let's see "**

BABE next to PREZ. PREZ starts slowly down to knees—figures on
floor. ALL gather around and lean over PREZ.

" That's two-hundred-and-sixty weeks . . . times forty hours a week . . . and at roughly two-and-a-quarter hours overtime at time and a half for overtime . . . come to exactly

ALL look at PREZ.

Eight-hundred and fifty-two dollars and seventy-four cents." [*Lifts head.*]

ALL [*Shout*]. Hurray. [*Break away—bodies up and arms shoot out.*]

PREZ [*Sings*]. That's enough for me to get
    An automatic washing machine, [*Reclining on floor face* S.R.'
    A year's supply of gasoline,
    Carpeting for the living room,

POOPSIE AND TWO GIRLS.
    A vacuum instead of a blasted broom.

PREZ. Not to mention a forty-inch television set [*Up half-way.*]

ALL So . . . although [*March—change places.*]

          BABE, PREZ *and* GIRL *link arms and skip to* S.L.
    Seven and a half cents doesn't buy a helluva lot
    Seven-and-a-half cents doesn't mean a thing,
    But give it to me every hour,
    Forty hours every week,
    That's enough for me to be
    Livin' like a king.

BABE [*Getting pad and pencil from* PREZ.]
    I figured it out, [*Goes* R.]

ALL.   She figured it out, [ALL *point at* BABE.]
    She figured it out, [*Use single arm to point.*]

BABE.   I figured it out, [*Goes* S.R.]
    With a pencil and a pad, [*Waves pencil in* R. *hand, pad in* L.]
    I figured it out, [*Waves both pencil and pad.*]
    Only ten years from today, [*Goes* S.R.]
    Only ten years from today, [*Goes* S.L.]
    I can see it clear as daylight
    Only ten years from today.

[*Spoken.*] " Ten years . . . now let's see . . . [*Picks up " Steam-Heat "* BOY, *leans on his back and figures.*] That's five-hundred-and-twenty weeks . . . times forty

          BOY *lifts* GIRL *on shoulder.*

hours every week . . . and roughly two-and-a-quarter hours overtime . . . at time-and-a-half for overtime—Comes to exactly one thousand seven hundred and five dollars and forty eight cents."

          ALL *cheer.*

[*Sings.*]   That's enough for me to buy

          BABE *lifted by* THREE BOYS.
    A trip to France across the seas, ⎫
    A motorboat and water skis, ⎬ [*In lift.*]
    Maybe even a foreign car. ⎭

THREE BOYS. A charge account at the corner bar.

BABE.   Not to mention a scrabble board with letters made of gold.

         BABE *down. Moves to* L.C.—*jumps in place*

ALL.   So . . . although [*March, change places.*]
    Seven-and-a-half cents doesn't buy a helluva lot,
    Seven-and-a-half cents doesn't mean a thing,

         BABE *goes* R.
    But give it to me every hour,
    Forty hours every week,
    That's enough for me to be
    Livin' like a king.

PREZ.   We figured it out.

         BABE *and* PREZ *to* C. *and out—she* R.—*he* L.

ALL.   They figured it out, [*On one knee, point one arm.*] They figured it out.
    [ALL *up, point one arm.*]

PREZ AND BABE.
    We figured it out! [*Meet and shake hands in* C. *and go out again— she* R.—*he* L.]

ALL.   With a pencil and a pad
    They figured it out.

         BABE S.R. PREZ S.L

BABE.   Only twenty years from today. [L. *hand out.*]

ALL.   Doooo-wah! [*Lean* R.]

PREZ [D.S.L.]. Only twenty years from today.

ALL.   Doooo-wah! [*Lean* L.]

BABE.   I can see it like a vision.

ALL.   Only twenty years from today—[*In* C.—*both.*]

PREZ [*Spoken.* C.].   **Twenty years. Now !et's see, that's one thousand**
Lifted by BOYS
and forty weeks . . . [*Cover lifts.*]
BABE [*Spoken. Lifted by* BOYS].   **Times forty hours every week.**
PREZ.   **And roughly two-and-a-quarter hours overtime at**
Lifted by BOYS.
BABE.   **Time-and-a-half for overtime,**
Lifted by BOYS.
PREZ.   **Comes to exactly . . .**
BABE.   **Three thousand, four hundred-and-eleven dollars** [*Face front—both
hands on head.*]
PREZ.   **And ninety-six cents.** [*Face front—both hands on head.*]
ALL [*Spoken. On knees*].   **Wow!**
Fall—sideways—back. PREZ *caught by* TWO BOYS. BABE *caught
by* ONE BOY.

PREZ [*Sings*].   **That's enough for me to be**
         A sultan in the Taj Mahal,
         In every room a different doll,
BABE [*Sings*]. [*Comes forward*].
         I'll have myself a buyin' spree,
         I'll buy a pajama factory,
         Then I could end up havin' old man Hasler work for me. [*Look
            of reaction.*]
ALL [*Sing*].   **So . . . although** [*March in place. All up.*]
         Seven-and-a-half cents doesn't buy a helluva lot,
                  PREZ *next to* BABE *front line.*
         Seven-and-a-half cents doesn't mean a thing,
         But give it to me [GIRLS *arms out open low.*]
         Every hour, [GIRLS *place hands on thighs.*]
         Forty hours [GIRLS *punch* R. *hand,* BOYS *punch* L. *hand.*]
         Every week, [BOYS *both arms high.*]
         That's enough for me to be [*On one knee—arms low, open.* BOYS
            bend knees and slowly up. Use arms as GIRLS.]
         Livin' like a king! [*Pulsate arms—higher and higher into pose on
            specific count.*]

                  BABE *lifted by* TWO BOYS. BOYS *catch* GIRLS, *on two open arms
                  —diagonally inside arm* H—S.R.—L. *high—*S.L.—R. *high.* PREZ
                  on floor at BABE'S *feet,* L. *arm high.*
                  SID *enters* D.L., *crosses to* L.C.

SID.   **Prez.**
PREZ.   **Yeah?**

                  HINES *sneaks on* L. *and lies masked by chorus.*

SID.   **We can settle this strike.**
PREZ.   **Well, how?**
SID.   **Sleep Tite can offer you a compromise.**
PREZ.   **What?**
SID.   **Mr. Hasler will give you the seven-and-a-half cents, if you give up the
claims for retroactive pay.**
MAE.   **We ain't giving up nothing.**
PREZ [*To* MAE].   **Now wait.** [*To* SID.] **Sid . . . I don't know.**
BABE.   **Well, I do. Let's get it over. We've won.**
BRENDA.   **We've won. We've won.**
JOE [*Running in* D.R.].   **Hasler's talking. He's at the rally.**
CROWD.   **Hurray!**
PREZ.   **Come on.**

Music 23A.   RUSH MUSIC

The CROWD *rushes out* R., *trampling* HINES.
HINES [*Rises, crosses* D.C.].   **I told you this show was full of symbolism.**
BABE.   **Oh, Sid.** [*Runs after* SID, *who is crossing* R., *and stops him*].   **I could kiss
you, you've been wonderful.** [*Standing* R. *of* SID.]
SID.   **I don't want to be kissed for settling a strike. Of course, if it's anything
personal . . .**
BABE.   **Oh, very personal.**
They kiss.

Music No. 24.   " THERE ONCE WAS A MAN " *Reprise*

HINES [*Sits down* C.]. [*Spoken*].   **Embarrassing, I call it.**

[Spoken].   Warn Cue 26, Flys and Traveller.

BABE. **I love you.**
SID. **Tell me.**
BABE. **I love you.**
SID. **Tell me.**
BABE. **I love you.**
SID. **Tell me more.**
BABE. **What a man. I'll tell you.**
[Sings.]   **More than a lion loves her cub,**
SID.   **More than a limey loves his pub,**
BABE.   **More than a flounder loves his fin,**   *[Flaps hands down at sides.]*
SID.   **More than a guzzler loves his gin,**   *[Drinks.]*
SID. **More,** BABE. **More,** SID. **More,** BABE. **More,** SID. **More,**
BABE.   **More,**
SID.   **More.**
                   There once was a man who loved a woman. *[High* R. *hand.]*
BABE.   **There once was a woman who loved a man,** *[*R. *hand to side.]*
SID.   **She was the one he slew the dragon for!** *[Points* R. *hand down.]*
BABE.   **He was the one that she took poison for!** *[Points* R. *hand down.]*
BOTH *[Both arms. Clasp self. Open arms].*
                   They say that nobody ever loved as much as { **he-ee,**
                                                                    { **shee-ee,**
                   But me-ee, I love you more.   *[Bring arm in to self crossed.]*
                   But me-ee, I love you more!
                                          SID *carries* BABE *off* D.R. HINES *rises and crosses to* C.

HINES *[Spoken].* **They'll never last!**

Music No. 25.   **" THE PAJAMA GAME "** *Closing*
                                          Black Drop away.
**And now we'll take you to one of the town's most exclusive clubs, where
a party was given jointly by Mr. Hasler and the Union. We were told to
dress for the occasion.**
                                          Cue 26, Traveller open fast.
                   HINES *exits* D.R.

FINALE

*The Traveller opens on Hernando's Hideaway, which is the Finale
set, and forms the second half of this scene.
The* BOYS *and* GIRLS *are dancing, (Jive dance) with the* SINGERS
U.S., *and the* DANCERS D.S.
When the Dance finishes SALESMAN *enters* D.L. *and crosses to* C.
The CROWD *take up positions around stage.*

(Music No. 25—continues)

SALESMAN *[Clapping his hands].* **Attention! Step back more . . . Quiet, quiet!**
HASLER *[Enters* D.R. *and crosses to* C.*].* **Now Max.**
SALESMAN. **Yes, M.H.**
HASLER. **I just want to say one word.**
SALESMAN. **Okay, M.H.**
HASLER. **Fellow Sleep Titers, this demonstration of harmony in our factory
   hits something deep inside of me and I know this party is going to be a
   great success because it stems from a genuine Sleep Tite spirit of
   solidarity.**
                   CROWD *applauds and* HASLER *crosses to* R.C. GIRL *kisses* HASLER
                   SALESMAN *crosses to* C.
SALESMAN. **Well, we sure all say Okay to that, M.H.** *[Crosses to* L.*]* **So on with
   out little tribute to Sleep Tite Pajamas. And now . . . on with the
   Sleep Tite Fashion parade.**
                                          Music Cue. (Fanfare).
Wear Sleep Tite at all social functions.
                   BOY *opens Centre Panel Curtains revealing* MABEL *clad in pajamas
                   She poses, then dances* D.C. *(4 slow steps, 4 fast steps in circle)—
                   and on cue says: (to music):*
MABEL. **Dresses are fine, but Sleep Tite's divine!** *[Crosses to* R., *sees* HASLER
   and acts embarrassed, joins group R.*]*
SALESMAN *[Spoken. Crossing to* L.C.*].* **Sleep Tite has everything, grace, style
   and comfort.**
BRENDA *[Appearing in opening. Crosses to* L.*].* **I'm grace.**
PREZ *[Appearing in opening. Crosses to* R.*].* **I'm style.**
MAE *[Appearing a. opening at* C.*].* **I'm comfort.**

They join crowd R. *and* L.   PREZ *to* R., BRENDA *and* MAE *to* L.

SALESMAN [*Crossing to* R.C.].   **Wear Sleep Tite for happy home life.**

Curtains open revealing GLADYS *and* HINES. *Two " Steam Heat '.*
BOYS *enter* D.R., *on cue and dance to* R.C. GLADYS *and* HINES
dance D.C., *and on cue* HINES *speaks.*

HINES [*Spoken, to music*].   **Now I trust her night and day; That's true love the**
Sleep Tite way.

GLADYS *moves to " Steam-Heat "* BOYS—HINES *pulls her back on*
chain to U.L.C. *" Steam-Heat "* BOYS *retire to* D.R.

SALESMAN [*Crosses to* L.].   **And another point. Sleep Tite is economical.**

Curtains open revealing SID *in pajama bottoms and* BABE *in*
pajama tops.

Warn House Tabs.

SID [*Spoken, to music. Coming* D.C.].   **Married life is lots of fun.**

BABE [*Coming* D.C.].   **Two can sleep as cheap as one.**

BOTH *cross* U.S.C.

BABE, SID AND ALL PRINCIPALS [*Sing. Feed into front line*].
The Pajama Game is the game we're in,
And we're proud to be in the Pajama Game.

ALL.   **We love it,**   [*Hold hands and come up.*]

Two by two going around each other S.L. *People going around* S.R.,
people on one knee. Hold hands—pump up and down R. *step-bend*
both knees L. *raised alternate.*

We can hardly wait to wake
And get to work at eight,   [*Let go hands.*]
Nothing's quite the same
As the Pajama Game.   [*Flip wrists out. Take position on last note.*]

" —same as the PajAMA game "—House Tabs in.

Positions when curtain falls :—
*Front row—Principals—*R. *to* L.*:—*

1ST *" Steam-Heat "* BOY, 2ND *" Steam-Heat "* BOY, HASLER,
MABEL, PREZ, GLADYS, SID, BABE, HINES, MAE, SALESMAN,
BRENDA, POP, CHARLIE.

Second row—Dancers in pairs—Matching pajamas. :—
Third row—Singers in pairs—Matching pajamas :—

When Curtain falls the Principals run offstage R. *and* L. *ready for*
individual calls. The Dancers and Singers remain on stage in two
rows. After the Curtain falls the Orchestra start the intro. to
" Seven-and-a-half Cents ".

Music No. 25A.   **" SEVEN-AND-A-HALF CENTS "**   *Reprise*

Count 4 of " Seven-and-a-half Cents " intro.—House Tabs. in.
The Company sing two choruses of " Seven-and-a-half Cents "
The BOYS *and* GIRLS *march on the spot, and the* PRINCIPALS *enter*
R. *and* L. *for individual calls in the following order—*
From stage R.*—*TWO *" Steam-Heat "* BOYS *and* POOPSIE.
From stage L.*—*SALESMAN, POP, CHARLIE.
From stage R.*—*BRENDA, PREZ, MAE.
From stage L.*—*HASLER, MABEL.
From stage R. *and* L. *together, respectively.—*SID, BABE, HINES
GLADYS.

ALL.   **So, although—**
Seven-and-a-half cents doesn't buy a helluva lot,
Seven-and-a-half cents doesn't mean a thing,
But give it to me ev'ry hour
Forty hours ev'ry week
And that's enough for me to be
Livin' like a King!
Livin' like a King.

Principals line stage R. *to* L.*:—*

1ST *" Steam-Heat "* BOY, 2ND *" Steam-Heat "* BOY, POOPSIE,
BRENDA, PREZ, MAE, SID, BABE, HINES, GLADYS, HASLER, MABEL,
SALESMAN, POP, CHARLIE.
On second " — living like a KING "—House Tabs in.

Ad lib. Calls.

Curtain up. Houselights for the National Anthem.

PLOTS

LIME PLOT
(4 Lamp Plot)

NO. 1 LAMP.

Act I.   Scene 1.   Prologue.
Nil.
Act I.   Scene 2.   Factory.
Pick up Gladys enters U.S. O.P. Open White. Follow to exit. Pick up Helpers enter U.S. P.S. Open White. Follow 1st Helper to exit. Pick up Gladys enters D.S. P.S. Open White. Follow to exit. Pick up Hines last entrance U.S. O.P. Open White. Fade on him as Stage lights fade at end of scene.
Act I.   Scene 3.   Elevator.
Pick up Individual Girls as they sing. Open White. Pick up Sid enters P.S. Open White. Follow to exit.
Act I.   Scene 4.   Office.
Pick up Gladys on 3 separate entrances U.S. P.S. Open White. Follow each time to exit.
Act I.   Scene 5.   Picnic Cross.
Pick up Brenda and Salesman, enter P.S. Open White. Follow to exit.
Act I.   Scene 6.   Picnic Scene.
Pick up Poopsie C. stage when she rings bell. Open White. Follow to exit. Pick up Poopsie enters D.S. O.P. Open White. Follow her until she goes U.S., then fade off. Pick up Mabel and Salesman as they join dance C. stage. Open White. Follow to exit. Pick up Mabel and Salesman enter D.S. O.P. Open White. Follow to exit.
Act I.   Scene 7.   Picnic Cross.
Pick up Prez enters O.P. Steel Blue. Black out on Cue.
Act I.   Scene 8.   Kitchen.
Nil.
Act I.   Scene 9.   Elevator.
Pick up Mae enters P.S. Open White. Spread on group with her D.S. Follow to exit.
Act I.   Scene 10.   Factory.
Pick up Gladys enters U.S. O.P. Open White. Follow to exit. Pick up Hines on 2 separate entrances U.S. O.P. Open White. Follow each time

INTERVAL

Act II.   Scene 1.   Eagle Hall.
Nil.
Steam Heat.
Pick up Prez enters D.S. O.P. for calls. Open White. Follow to exit.
Act II.   Scene 2.   Kitchen.
Pick up Babe D.R. Open White. Follow until No. 3 Lamp takes over, then fade off.
Act II.   Scene 3.   Tick Tock.
Pick up Salesman enters P.S. Open White. Follow to exit.
Act II.   Scene 4.   Office.
Pick up Salesman enters U.S. O.P. Open White. Follow him until Gladys enters U.S. P.S. then pick her up. When Gladys finishes speaking pick up Salesman again, and follow to exit. Pick up Gladys again after Salesman exits. Follow to exit.
Act II.   Scene 4(a).   Hernando's Cross.
Nil.
Act II.   Scene 5.   Hernando's Hideaway.
Pick up Prez at table D.R. when Sid speaks to him. Open White. Follow to exit.
Act II.   Scene 5(a).   Jealousy Ballet.
Nil.
Intermediate Scene.   Strip.
Pick up Hines enters D.S. O.P. Open White. Follow to exit.
Act II.   Scene 6.   Office.
Pick up Hines standing in doorway U.S. O.P. Open White. Follow to exit. Pick up Hines enters U.S. O.P. Open White. Follow to exit.
Act II.   Scene 7.   Seven-and-a-Half Cents.
Pick up Prez enters D.S. O.P. Open White. Follow to exit. Pick up Hines standing D.L. after Prez exits. Open White. Follow to exit.
Finale.
Pick up Salesman enters D.S. P.S. Open White. Follow until line-up for " Pajama Game " then Flood stage. Flood company for Calls, O.P. side of stage. Open White.

NO. 2 LAMP.

Act I. Scene 1. Prologue.
   Nil.
Act I. Scene 2. Factory.
   Pick up Hasler enters U.S. O.P. Open White. Follow to exit. Pick up Hines enters D.S. P.S. Open White. Follow to exit. Pick up Singing Boy I and Girl C. stage. Open White. Fade off as they separate. Pick up Singing Boy II and 2nd Helper C. stage. Open White. Fade off as they separate. Pick up Hines enters U.S. O.P. Open White. Follow to exit. Pick up Sid enters U.S. P.S. Open White. Head and shoulders pin-spot for " Blue Town." Spread for dialogue sequence. Head and shoulders pin-spot for rest of " Blue Town." Spread on Sid at end of " Blue Town " and follow to exit.
Act I. Scene 3. Elevator.
   Pick up Babe enters D.S. O.P. Open White, small spot. Fade off with stage lights as she exits.
Act I. Scene 4. Office.
   Pick up Hines enters U.S. O.P. Open White. Follow to exit. Pick up Sid enters U.S. O.P. Open White. Fade off with stage lights.
Act I. Scene 5. Picnic Cross.
   Nil.
Act I. Scene 6. Picnic.
   Pick up Sid walking D.S. to Babe D.L., after opening number. Open White. Follow until Salesman starts announcing. Pick up Salesman C. stage when he starts announcing. Open White. Fade off when Hines prepares to throw knives. Pick up Sid D.R. after Mabel faints. Open White. Follow to exit. Pick up Sid enters D.S. O.P. Open White. Follow to exit.
Act I. Scene 7. Picnic Cross.
   Pick up Charlie enters O.P. Steel Blue. Follow to exit.
Act I. Scene 8. Kitchen.
   Pick up Babe enters P.S. Open White. Pin-spot for " Small Talk," and reprise at end of scene. Fade off with stage lights.
Act I. Scene 9. Elevator.
   Pick up Babe enters P.S. Open White. Follow to exit.
Act I. Scene 10. Factory.
   Pick up Prez enters U.S. O.P. Open White. Spread on Prez and group D.L. Follow Prez to exit. Pick up Sid enters U.S. O.P. Open White. Fade out with Tabs.

INTERVAL

Act II. Scene 1. Eagle Hall.
   Nil.
Steam Heat.
   Pick up Boy standing L. in trio C. stage. Open White. Follow to exit, then pick him up for first call and stand by to pick him up again on Cue from Prompt Corner.
Act II. Scene 2. Kitchen.
   Pick up Mae sitting at table. Open White. Follow to exit. Pick up Sid enters C. Open White. Fade off with Kitchen lights.
Act II. Scene 3. Tick Tock.
   Pick up Hines enters O.P. Open White. B.O. on Cue.
Act II. Scene 4. Office.
   Pick up Hasler enters U.S. O.P. Open White. Follow to exit.
Act II. Scene 4(a). Hernando's Cross.
   Pick up Man in Cloak enters O.P. Open White. Follow to exit.
Act II. Scene 5. Hernando's Hideaway.
   Pick up Prez enters D.S. O.P. Open White. Fade off when he sits at table D.R. Pick up Sid as he stands up C. as Babe crosses to him. Open White. Follow to exit. After Sid exits spread on aperture in truck above Gladys head to pick up Mae. Follow Mae to exit.
Act II. Scene 5(a). Jealousy Ballet.
   Pick up Gladys enters D.S. O.P. Open White. Stay on Gladys.
Intermediate Scene. Strip.
   Stay on Gladys. Open White. Follow to exit.
Act II. Scene 6. Office.
   Pick up Babe enters U.S. O.P. Open White. Spread on her and Prez and Joe. When Prez and Joe exit stay on Babe and follow to exit. Pick up Gladys enters U.S. P.S. Open White. Follow to exit.
Act II. Scene 7. Seven-and-a-Half Cents.
   Pick up Babe enters O.P. Open White. Follow to exit.
Finale.
   Pick up Hasler enters D.S. O.P. Open White. Follow to end of speech then fade off. Pick

up Brenda enters C. stage. Open White. Fade off as she joins group. Pick up 2 Steam Heat Boys enter D.S. O.P. Open White. Fade off as they join group. Flood stage on line-up for "Pajama Game." Open White.

Curtain Calls.

Flood stage P. side. Open White.

NO. 3 LAMP.

Act I. Scene 1. Prologue.

Nil.

Act I. Scene 2. Factory.

Pick up Prez enters D.S. P.S. Open White. Follow to exit. Pick up Mabel enters D.S. P.S. Open White. Follow to exit. Strip on Girls at bench for "Racing with the Clock." Open White. Fade off at end of number. Pick up Charlie enters U.S. P.S. Open White. Follow to exit. Pick up Hines enters D.S. P.S. Open White. Follow to exit. Pick up Mabel enters D.S. P.S. Open White. Follow to exit.

Act I. Scene 3. Elevator.

Pick up Prez enters D.S. P.S. Open White. Follow to exit. Strip Girls R. stage for number. Pink. Fade off at end of number.

Act I. Scene 4. Office.

Pick up Poopsie enters U.S. O.P. Open White. Follow to exit. Pick up Hasler enters U.S. O.P. Open White. Follow to exit. Pick up Hasler enters U.S. P.S. Open White. Follow to exit. Pick up Babe enters U.S. O.P. Open White. Follow to exit.

Act I. Scene 5. Picnic Cross.

Pick up Poopsie enters P.S. Open White. Follow to exit. Pick up Mae enters P.S. Open White. Follow to exit. Pick up Gladys enters P.S. Open White. B.O. on Cue.

Act I. Scene 6. Picnic.

Pick up Hines when he stands up at R. table with bottle in hand. Open White. Fade off when he sits down. Pick up Babe standing D.L. Open White. Fade off when she crosses to D.S. of knife board. Spot knife board when Poopsie swoons. Open White. Pick up Babe when she stands in front of knife board. Open White. Follow to exit. Pick up Poopsie running in to C. from D.L. for solo line. Open White. Follow to exit. Pick up Gladys D.R. when crowd yells her name. Open White. Follow her until stops dancing U.S. and joins group, then fade off. Pick up Gladys when she is lifted above group of dancers at C. stage. Open White. Fade off as she goes down. Pick up Prez when he is lifted above group of dancers at C. stage. Open White. Fade off as he goes down. Pick up Gladys C. stage as boys separate in front of her. Open White. Follow her. B.O. on Cue.

Act I. Scene 7. Picnic Cross.

Pick up Mabel enters D.S. O.P. Steel Blue. Follow to exit. Pick up Mae enters D.S. O.P. Steel Blue. Follow to exit. B.O. on Cue.

Act I. Scene 8. Kitchen.

Pick up Sid sitting R. of R. table. Open White. Pin-spot on Sid for number "Small Talk." Spread at end of number. Pin-spot on Sid when Babe starts singing reprise of "Small Talk." Fade off with stage lights.

Act I. Scene 9. Elevator.

Pick up Sid enters D.S. P.S. Open White. Follow to exit.

Act I. Scene 10. Factory.

Pick up Mabel enters D.S. O.P. Open White. Follow to exit. Pick up Hasler enters U.S. O.P. Open White. Follow to exit. Pick up Mae after Hasler's exit. Open White. Follow her until she moves up to bench then fade off.

INTERVAL

Act II. Scene 1. Eagle Hall.

Nil.

Steam Heat.

Pick up Gladys standing C. of trio U.S. C. Open White. Follow to exit. Pick up Gladys as she re-enters D.S. O.P. for call. Stand by to pick her up again on Cue from Prompt Corner.

Act II. Scene 2. Kitchen.

Pick up Prez standing at R. table. Open White. Follow to exit. Pick up Babe standing stage R. after exit of Prez. Open White. Follow to exit. Pick up Babe coming through Curtains D.S. L. on Cue from Corner. Open White. Pin-spot. Fade off on Cue.

Act II. Scene 3. Tick Tock.

Nil.

Act II. Scene 4. Office.

Pick up Sid sitting at desk R. stage. Open White. Follow to exit. Pick up Mabel after Sid's exit. Open White. Follow her until she crosses to L. desk, then fade off. Pick up Sid enters U.S. O.P. Open White. Follow him.

Act II.   Scene 4(a).   *Hernando's Cross.*
  Change to Steel Blue and stay on Sid.   Follow to exit.   Pick up Dwarf enters D.S. O.P.
  Steel Blue.   Follow to exit.   When Dwarf exits P.S. keep spot on edge of portal to Pick up
  3 Boys' arms then heads.   B.O. on Cue.
Act II.   Scene 5.   *Hernando's Hideaway.*
  Pick up Gladys and Sid sitting C. stage, after finish of " Hernando's Hideaway " number.
  Steel Blue.   When Sid and Gladys separate follow Gladys to exit.
Act II.   Scene 5(a).   *Jealousy Ballet.*
  Nil.
Intermediate Scene.   Strip.
  Strip Dancing Boys when they come D.S.   Open White.   Stay on group R. stage.   When
  they dive to C. stage cut off.   Pick up Mabel (Angel) enters D.S. O.P.   Open White.   B.O.
  on Cue.
Act II.   Scene 6.   *Office.*
  Pick up Sid sitting at R. desk.   Open White.   Follow to exit.   Pick up Sid enters U.S. O.P.
  Open White.   B.O. on Cue.
Act II.   Scene 7.   *Seven-and-a-Half Cents.*
  Strip Groups R. stage at start of " Seven-and-a-Half Cents " number.   Open White.   Cut
  off at end of number.   Pick up Sid enters D.S. P.S.   Open White.   Follow to exit.
Finale.
  Strip Dancers R. stage.   Open White.   Cut off at end of dance.   Pick up Mabel enters C.
  stage.   Open White.   Follow until she joins group D.R. then fade off.   Pick up Prez enters
  C. stage.   Open White.   Follow until he joins group D.R. then fade off.   Pick up Hines
  enters C. stage.   Open White.   Follow until he joins group L.C. stage, then fade off.   Pick
  up Babe enters C. stage.   Open White.   Follow her until Principals come D.S. for " Pajama
  Game," then Flood C. stage.
Curtain Calls.
  Pick up Principals as they enter D.S. O.P. for their calls.   Fade off each after they take their
  bow.   Flood C. stage for final line-up.

NO. 4 LAMP.

Act I.   Scene 1.   *Prologue.*
  Pick up Hines enters D.S. O.P.   Open White.   Follow him.
Act I.   Scene 2.   *Factory.*
  Stay on Hines.   Open White.   Follow to exit.   Strip on Groups of Boys and Girls on R.
  stage as they form up at end of " Racing with the Clock."   Fade off as they break up after
  number.   Pick up Mabel enters U.S. O.P.   Open White.   Follow to exit.   Pick up 2nd
  Helper standing D.R. after Mabel's exit.   Open White.   Follow to exit.   Pick up Hasler
  enter D.S. P.S.   Open White.   Follow to exit.   Pick up Babe enters D.S. P.S.   Open White.
  Follow to exit.
Act I.   Scene 3.   *Elevator.*
  Strip on Girls L. stage at start of number " I'm not at all in Love."   Pink.   Fade off at
  end of number.
Act I.   Scene 4.   *Office.*
  Pick up Mabel sitting at L. desk.   Open White.   Follow to exit.
Act I.   Scene 5.   *Picnic Cross.*
  Pick up Prez enters D.S. P.S.   Open White.   Follow to exit.
Act I.   Scene 6.   *Picnic.*
  Pick up Prez when he makes a speech on L. table.   Open White.   Stay on him until he
  introduces Hasler then—Pick up Hasler on L. table.   Stay on him until he finishes speech
  then—Pick up Prez on L. table.   Fade off when he jumps off table.   Pick up Prez and Brenda
  standing D.L. after speeches on table.   Open White.   Follow to exit.   Pick up Brenda
  enters D.S. P.S.   Open White.   Stay on her until knife-throwing announcement then fade
  off.   Pick up Hines R.C. stage for knife-throwing.   Open White.   Follow to exit.
Act I.   Scene 7.   *Picnic Cross.*
  Pick up Salesman enters D.S. O.P.   Steel Blue.   Follow to exit.
Act I.   Scene 8.   *Kitchen.*
  Pick up Pop sitting L. of R. table.   Open White.   Follow to exit.   Pick up Pop enters P.S.
  Open White.   Follow to exit.
Act I.   Scene 9.   *Elevator.*
  Pick up Prez enters D.S. P.S.   Open White.   Follow to exit.
Act I.   Scene 10.   *Factory.*
  Pick up Babe enters D.S. P.S.   Open White.   Follow her until she sits at bench then fade
  off.   Pick up Babe at bench when she stands up.   Open White.   Follow to exit.

INTERVAL

Act II. Scene 1. *Eagle Hall.*
Pick up Prez enters D.S. O.P. Open White. Follow to exit.
Steam Heat.
Pick up " Steam Heat " Boy standing R. in trio C. stage. Open White. Follow to exit.
Pick up Boy as he enters D.S. O.P. for call. Stand by to pick up Boy again on Cue from Prompt Corner.
Act II. Scene 2. *Kitchen.*
Pick up Pop enters C. stage. Follow to exit. Open White. Pick up Brenda and Joe at R. stage after Pop's exit. Open White. Follow to exit. Pick up Pop enters P.S. Open White. Follow to exit.
Act II. Scene 3. *Tick Tock.*
Nil.
Act II. Scene 4. *Office.*
Pick up Mabel seated at L. desk. Open White. Follow her until entrance of Salesman, then fade off. Pick up Hines enters U.S. O.P. Open White. Follow to exit. Pick up Gladys enters U.S. O.P. after Hines' exit. Open White. Follow her and stand by to change colour to Steel Blue for next scene.
Act II. Scene 4(a). *Hernando's Cross.*
Stay on Gladys and change to Steel Blue. Follow to exit.
Act II. Scene 5. *Hernando's Hideaway.*
Pick up Babe enters D.S. O.P. Steel Blue. Follow to exit. Pick up Hines enters U.S. P.S. Steel Blue. Follow him into next scene.
Act II. Scene 5(a). *Jealousy Ballet.*
Stay on Hines. Steel Blue. Follow him for his three entrances in scene.
Intermediate Scene. Strip.
Strip Dancing Boys when they come D.S. Open White. Stay on group L. stage. When they dive to C. stage cover all of them. Follow to exit.
Act II. Scene 6. *Office.*
Pick up Charlie enters U.S. O.P. Open White. Follow to exit. Pick up Hasler enters U.S. P.S. Open White. B.O. on Cue.
Act II. Scene 7. *Seven-and-a-Half Cents.*
Strip Groups L. stage at start of " Seven-and-a-Half Cents " number. Open White. Cut off at end of Number.
Finale.
Strip Dancers L. stage. Open White. Cut off at end of dance. Pick up Mae C. stage. Open White. Follow until she joins group L. stage then fade off. Pick up Gladys enters C. stage. Open White. Follow until she joins group L. stage then fade off. Pick up Sid enters C. stage. Open White. Follow until line-up for " Pajama Game," then Flood C. stage.
Curtain Calls.
Pick up Principals as they enter D.S. P.S. for their calls. Fade off each after they take their bow. Flood C. stage for final line-up.

$$\boxed{\text{LIGHTING PLOT}}$$

Verbal Cue.
Beginning of Overture. Circle Spots—Amber and Lavender/Blue Full. Box Pageants—1 lamp each side Full. Floats—Amber, Pink and Blue circuits Full.
Verbal Cue.
End of " Small Talk " in Overture—House Lights Out.
Pre-set. Act I. Scene 1. Prologue.
No. 1 Batt.—Pink and Blue circuits at ½. No. 1 A.A. Bar—Ambers Full. No. 1 Boom—Ambers and Blues Full.
Cue 2. " This play is full of SYMBOLISM."
Fade all to ½ (Count of 6).
Cue 2a. " I'm an EXECUTIVE."
Fade all to B.O. (Count of 6).
Cue 3. " O.K. let her GO."
No. 2 Batt.—Blue circuit Full. No. 3 Batt.—Blue circuit Full. No. 4 Batt.—Pink and Blue circuits Full. No. 5 Batt.—Pink and Blue circuits Full. No. 2 A.A. Bar—Amber and Blue circuits Full. No. 3 Pageant Bar—Amber and Blue circuits Full. No. 1 Ladder—Amber and Blue lamps Full. No. 2 Ladder—Amber and Blue lamps Full. 2 Kw. Spot on stand P. side shining across machine bench—Full. 2 Kw. Spot on stand O.P. side shining through O.P. window—Full. Ground rows—All circuits Blue, Full. Follow on with: Circle Spots—Amber and Lavender/Blue Full. Box Pageants—All Full. Floats—All circuits Full. No. 1 Boom—Amber and Blue Full. No. 1 A.A. Bar—Amber and Blue lamps Full. No. 1 Batt.—Amber, Pink and Blue circuits Full. Sewing machine pendants Full.
Cue 5. " — MOVE."
Fade all to ¾ (Count of 3).
Cue 6. " — ain't gonna LICK me."
Raise all to Full (Count of 3).
Cue 8. " — it's a losing RACE."
Fade all to B.O. (Count of 2).
Working-lights on.
Cue 9. When Elevator Cloth in.
Circle Spots—Amber and Lavender/Blue Full. Floats—All circuits to ½. No. 1 A.A. Bar—All Ambers and Blues to Full. No. 1 Boom—All Ambers and Blues to Full.
Cue 10. " — sure of himself for ME."
Floats—All circuits to Full.
Working-lights out.
Cue 11. On Music pick-up after applause.
Fade all to B.O. (Count of 6).
Cue 12. When Elevator Cloth away and desk set.
Fade in Count of 4. Circle Spots—6 to 19—Amber, Pink and Blue Full. Floats—C. Sections only—Amber, Pink and Blue to ½. No. 2 Batt.—White and Blue circuits to ½. No. 3 Batt.—White, Amber, Pink and Blue circuits to ½. No. 1 Spot Bar—Office Spots Full. No. 2 Spot Bar—Office Spots Full. No. 1 Ladder—O.P. side—Single Amber lamp shining on translucency above office door—Full. 1-2 Kw. Spot on stand O.P.—Shining on Office back-cloth—½. 1 Amber Flood on stand shining on back of P. office door—½.
Cue 13. " THAT'S easier said than done."
Fade all to ½ (Count of 4).
Cue 13a. " — never be jealous AGAIN."
Fade all to Mark 3—Scale of 10 (Count of 4).
Cue 14. When Hines seats Mabel on chair.
Raise all to Full (Count of 4).
Cue 15. " HEY there."
Fade all to ½ (Count of 4).
Cue 16. " — and out THE other."
Fade all to B.O. (Count of 4).
Working-lights on.
Cue 17. When Picnic Gauze and Black Drop in.
Fade in quickly: Circle Spots—All Amber, Pink and Blue to Full. Box Pageants—All to Full. Floats—Amber, Pink and Blue circuits to Full. No. 1 Batt.—Pink and Blue circuits to Full. No. 1 A.A. Bar—All Ambers and Blues to Full. No. 1 Boom—All Ambers and Blues to Full.
Working-lights out.
Cue 18. When Gladys at Portal.
Fade all to B.O. (Count of 4).
Cue 19. Start of " Sleep Tite " intro.
Fade in quickly: No. 2 Batt.—White and Blue circuits to Full. No. 3 Batt.—Amber, Pink and

Blue circuits to Full.   No. 4 Batt.—Pink and Blue circuits to Full.   No. 5 Batt.—Pink and Blue circuits to Full.   No. 2 A.A. Bar—All Ambers and Blues to Full.   No. 3 Pageant Bar—All Ambers and Blues to Full.   No. 1 Ladder—All Ambers and Blues to Full.   No. 2 Ladder—All Ambers and Blues to Full.   1-2 Kw. Spot on Stand P. side Full—Shining across L. table.   1-2 Kw. Spot on stand O.P. Full—Shining across R. table.   Groundrows—All circuits Full.   Follow on with: Circle Spots—Amber and Lavender/Blue to Full.   Box Pageants—All to Full.   Floats—Amber, Pink and Blue circuits to Full.   No. 1 Batt.—Amber, Pink and Blue circuits to Full.   No. 1 Boom—All Ambers and Blues to Full.   No. 1 A.A. Bar—All Ambers and Blues to Full.

Cue 23.   *" THIS is my once a year day."*
Circle Spots—Centre 8 Lamps (Autos)—Change to Pale Lemon.

Cue 24.   *When 3 Solo dancers pop up.*
D.B.O.

Working-lights on.

Cue 25.   *When Picnic Gauze and Black Drop in.*
Fade in quickly: Circle Spots—All Blue circuits to Full.   Floats—Blue circuit to Full.   No. 1 Batt.—Blue circuit to Full.   No. 1 A.A. Bar—All Blues to Full.   No. 1 Boom—All Blues to Full.

Working-light out.

Cue 26.   *When Mae pulls Prez off L.*
Fade to B.O. (Count of 4).

Cue 27.   *When Picnic Gauze 12' high.*
Fade in (Count of 4): No. 3 Batt.—Blue circuit to Full.   No. 4 Batt.—Blue circuits to Full.   No. 5 Batt.—Blue circuits to Full.   Signal lights to mark 2.   Follow on with (Count of 4): Circle Spots—C. 8 Lamps (Autos)—Amber and Lavender/Blue to Full.   No. 1 Spot Bar—Kitchen spots to Full.   No. 2 Spot Bar—Kitchen spot to Full.   Strips below windows to Full.   Baby Spot on stand O.P.—Full—Shining on back of House Piece Panel in O.P. Portal.

Cue 28.   *Beginning of " Small Talk."*
Fade all except Battens and Signal Lights to $\frac{1}{2}$ (Count of 4).

Cue 29.   *Tacit: " And that TAKES no talk at all."*
Raise all except Battens and Signal lights to Full (Count of 4).

Cue 30.   *When Sid and Babe nearly sit in chair.*
Fade all except Battens and Signal lights to B.O. (Count of 4).   Follow on with: Fade all Battens and Signal lights to B.O. (Count of 4).

Working-lights on.

Cue 30a.   *When Elevator Cloth in.*
Fade in quickly: Circle Spots—Lavender/Blue to Full.   Floats—Amber, Pink and Blue circuits to Full.   No. 1 A.A. Bar—All Ambers and Blues to Full.   No. 1 Boom—All Ambers and Blues to Full.

Cue 30b.   *Beginning of " Once was a Man."*
Fade all to $\frac{1}{2}$ (Count of 4).

Working-lights out.

Cue 30c.   *As Sid carries Babe off L.*
Fade all quickly to B.O.

Cue 33.   *When Elevator Cloth away.*
Fade in quickly: Circle Spots—Amber and Lavender/Blue to Full.   Box Pageants—All to Full.   Floats—Amber, Pink and Blue circuits to Full.   No. 1 Batt.—Amber, Pink and Blue circuits to Full.   No. 2 Batt.—Blue circuits to Full.   No. 3 Batt.—Blue circuits to Full.   No. 4 Batt.—Pink and Blue circuits to Full.   No. 5 Batt.—Pink and Blue circuits to Full.   No. 1 A.A. Bar—All Ambers and Blues to Full.   No. 2 A.A. Bar—All Ambers and Blues to Full.   No. 3 Pageant Bar—All Ambers and Blues to Full.   No. 1 Boom—All Ambers and Blues to Full.   No. 1 Ladder—All Ambers and Blues to Full.   No. 2 Ladder—All Ambers and Blues to Full.   Sewing machine pendants to Full.   Ground rows—All circuits to Full.   1-2 Kw. Spot on stand O.P. Full—Shining through R. window.   1-2 Kw. Spot on stand P. Full—Shining across bench.

Cue 35.   *" BETTER forget her."*
Fade all to $\frac{3}{4}$ (Count of 4).

Verbal Cue when House Tabs are down.
House lights on.

INTERVAL

Pre-set.   Act II.   Scene 1.   Eagle Hall.
No. 2 Batt.—Blue circuit Full.   No. 1 A.A. Bar—Ambers and Blues $\frac{1}{2}$.   No. 1 Boom—Ambers and Blues $\frac{1}{2}$.

Verbal Cue.
Start of Entracte.   Circle Spots—3 C. lamps Blue $\frac{1}{2}$.   2 C. lamps Lavender $\frac{1}{2}$.   Floats—Amber, Pink and Blue $\frac{1}{2}$—C. section only.

Verbal Cue.
End of " Hey There " in Entracte—House Lights out.
Cue 1a. *" — that's what we're DOING."*
Count of 3 Cross Fade to: Circle Spots—Blues Full. Floats—Blue circuit Full. No. 1 Boom—2 top Amber lamps each side only—Full.
Cue 1b. *On 2nd " But that don't do no GOOD."*
Fade all to B.O. (Count of 3).
Cue 1c. *On MUSIC pick-up after Clap section.*
Fade in (Count of 3): Circle Spots—Blues Full. Floats—Blue circuits Full. No. 1 A.A. Bar—Blues Full.
Cue 1d. *On SCREAM and slide.*
Fade in quickly: Circle Spots—Ambers and Pinks to $\frac{1}{2}$. Box Pageants—All to $\frac{1}{2}$. Floats— Amber, Pink and Blue circuits to $\frac{1}{2}$. No. 1 Boom—Ambers and Blues to $\frac{1}{2}$. No. 1 A.A. Bar—Ambers to $\frac{1}{2}$.
Cue 2. *As PREZ exits D.R.*
Fade all to B.O. (Count of 3).
Cue 3. *When Kitchen Truck set.*
Fade in (Count of 3): No. 3 Batt.—Blue circuit Full. No. 4 Batt.—Blue circuit Full. No. 5 Batt.—Blue circuit Full. Signal Lights to mark 2. Follow on (Count of 3): Circle Spots— C. 8 lamps—Amber and Lavender/Blue Full. No. 1 Spot Bar—Kitchen Spots Full. No. 2 Spot Bar—Kitchen Spot Full. Strips below windows Full. Baby Spot on stand O.P. Full— Shining on back of House Piece Panel in O.P. Portal.
Cue 3a. *" Pan American ISSUES."*
Fade all except Battens and Signal Lights to out. (Count of 6.)
Cue 4. *" — are you too much in LOVE."*
Fade all to B.O. (Count of 4).
Working-lights on.
Cue 5. *When Elevator Cloth in and last chord of music.*
Fade in quickly: Circle Spots—Lavender and Blue Full. Floats—All circuits Full. No. 1 Boom—All Ambers and Blues Full. No. 1 A.A. Bar—Ambers and Blues Full.
Working-lights out.
Cue 6. *When Hines raises hat.*
D.B.O.
Cue 7. *When Elevator Cloth away and desk set.*
Fade in quickly: Circle Spots—6, 7, 17, 18, 19—Amber and Lavender/Blue Full. 8 to 16— White Full. Floats—All circuits to $\frac{1}{2}$. No. 2 Batt.—White and Blue circuits Full. No. 3 Batt.—Amber, Pink and Blue circuits Full. White circuit to $\frac{1}{2}$. No. 1 Spot Bar—Office Spots Full. No. 2 Spot Bar—Office Spots Full. No. 1 Ladder—O.P. side—Single Amber lamp shining on translucency above R. office door—Full. 1-2 Kw. Spot on stand O.P. at $\frac{1}{2}$. Shining on office backcloth. 1 Amber Flood on stand at $\frac{1}{2}$. Shining on back of L. office door.
Cue 8. *" I know a wonderful JOINT."*
Fade all to B.O. (Count of 4).
Cue 9. *When Traveller nearly closed.*
Fade in (Count of 4): No. 1 Boom—Ambers and Blues Full.
Cue 9a. *" — but not my KEY."*
Fade in (Count of 6): Circle Spots—Blues to $\frac{1}{2}$. Floats—Amber circuit to $\frac{1}{2}$. No. 1 Batt.— Ambers and Blue circuits to $\frac{1}{2}$.
Working-lights on.
Working-lights out when scene set.
Cue 10. *" Joe sent US."*
D.B.O. And Switch on: Sign Cloth—" Hernando's Hideaway," " Chop Suey," Red arrows.
Cue 11. *On Music change.*
Switch off—" Hernando's Hideaway " and " Chop Suey." Follow on when Cloth going away—Switch off Red arrows.
Cue 12. *" Then strike a match and you will KNOW."*
Snap in: Circle Spots—All Amber and Lavender/Blue to $\frac{1}{2}$. Floats—Blue circuit to $\frac{1}{2}$. No. 2 Batt.—Blue circuit to $\frac{3}{4}$. No. 4 Batt.—Blue circuit to Full. No. 5 Batt.—Blue circuit to Full. No. 1 A.A. Bar—1 Amber lamp extreme R. to mark 2. No. 2 A.A. Bar—Blues to $\frac{1}{2}$. No. 1 Boom—Ambers and Blues to $\frac{1}{2}$. Hanging Lanterns to mark 4. 3 Neon Signs U.S. of Win- dows to $\frac{1}{2}$. Juke Box light to $\frac{1}{2}$.
Cue 13. *After applause for number.*
Fade all Circle Spots out (Count of 3).
Cue 14. *" I CAN see what marriage with Gladys — "*
Fade all to B.O. (Count of 4).
Cue 15. *When Hideaway trucks half open.*
Fade in (Count of 4): Circle Spots—C. 8 lamps—Pale Lemon—Full. Floats—Blue circuit Full. No. 2 Batt.—Blue circuit Full. No. 3 Batt.—Blue circuit Full. No. 4 Batt.—White and Blue circuit Full. No. 6 Batt.—Amber circuit to mark 7. No. 2 Spot Bar—4 Spots Full.

Cue 20.　*COUNT* 18 *of music of boys out of cupboard.*
　　　Cross Fade all in Cue 15 to—(Count of 6): Circle Spots—Blue lamps to Full.　Floats—Amber circuit to Full.　No. 1 Batt.—Blue circuit to Full.

Working-lights on.
Working-lights out when scene set.
Cue 21.　*As Angel exits Off L.*
　　　D.B.O.
Cue 22.　*When Black Drop away.*
　　　Fade in quickly: Circle Spots—6, 7, 17, 18, 19—Amber and Lavender/Blue Full.　8 to 16— White Full.　Floats—All circuits to ½.　No. 2 Batt.—White and Blue circuits Full.　No. 3 Batt.—Amber, Pink and Blue circuits Full.　White circuit to ½.　No. 1 Spot Bar—Office Spots Full.　No. 2 Spot Bar—Office Spots Full.　No. 1 Ladder—O.P. side—Single Amber lamp shining on translucency above R. office door—Full.　1-2 Kw. Spot on stand O.P. at ½. Shining on office backcloth.　1 Amber Flood on stand at ½.　Shining on back of L. office door.
Cue 23.　*" I'll break IT."*
　　　Fade in (Count of 4): Circle Spots—22 and 23—Full.　Box Pageants— 1 lamp O.P. to Full.
Cue 24.　*" — sit down and talk to ME."*
　　　D.B.O.
Cue 25.　*When Traveller nearly closed.*
　　　Fade in (Count of 4): Circle Spots—All Amber and Lavender/Blue Full.　Box Pageants— All Full.　Floats—All circuits Full.　No. 1 Boom—All Ambers and Blues Full.　No. 1 A.A. Bar—All Ambers Full.
Working-lights on.
Working-lights out when scene set.
Cue 26.　*" — dress for the OCCASION."*
　　　Fade in quickly No. 1 A.A. Bar—All Blues Full.　Hanging Lanterns to Full.　3 Neon Signs U.S. of windows to Full.　Change 8 C. Circle Spots to Pale Lemon.
Verbal Cue for House-lights when House Tabs raised for Anthem.

CUE SHEET

Check the following:—

    House Tabs in.   Traveller closed.   Black Drop in.   No. 1 Batt. Pilots off.
5 mins. before start of Overture.
    Call Overture and Beginners.   Ring Orchestra in.
1 min. before Overture.
    Send M.D. in.
Start of Overture.
    Ring 3 bar bells.   Verbal Cue to Elecs.   Circle Spots—Amber and Lavender/Blue to Full. Box Pageants—1 each side Full.   Floats—Amber, Pink and Blue circuits Full.
Check the following:—
    Factory Scene set.   Girls on stage.   Panels clear.   Hines O.P.
Pre-set Act I.   Scene 1.   Prologue.
    No. 1 Batt.—Pink and Blue circuits to $\frac{1}{2}$.   No. 1 A.A. Bar—Ambers Full.   No. 1 Boom— Ambers and Blues Full.
Verbal Cue end of " Small Talk " in Overture.
    House Lights out.
Working-lights out.
Fly House Tabs at end of applause for Overture.
Cue 2.   " This play is full of SYMBOLISM."
    Fade all to $\frac{1}{2}$ (Count of 6).
Cue 2a.   " I'm an EXECUTIVE."
    Fade all to B.O. (Count of 6).
Fly Black Drop away when lights out.
Cue 3 and Open Traveller fast on " O.K. let her GO."
    No. 2 Batt.—Blue circuit Full.   No. 3 Batt.—Blue circuit Full.   No. 4 Batt.—Pink and Blue circuits Full.   No. 5 Batt.—Pink and Blue circuits Full.   No. 2 A.A. Bar—Ambers and Blues Full.   No. 3 Pageant Bar—Ambers and Blues Full.   No. 1 Ladder—Ambers and Blues Full.   No. 2 Ladder— Ambers and Blues Full.   2 Kw. Spot on stand P. Full—Shining across bench.   2 Kw. Spot on stand O.P. Full—Shining through R. window.   Ground rows—All circuits Full.   Follow on with: Circle Spots—Amber and Lavender/Blue Full.   Box Pageants —All Full.   Floats—All circuits Full.   No. 1 Boom—Ambers and Blues Full.   No. 1 A.A. Bar—Ambers and Blues Full.   No. 1 Batt.—Amber, Pink and Blue Circuits Full.   Sewing machine pendants Full.
Cue Factory Gong at end of " Racing with the Clock."
Cue 5.   Start of " New Town."
    Fade all to $\frac{3}{4}$ (Count of 3).
Cue 6.   End of " New Town."
    Raise all to Full (Count of 3).
Cue Factory Gong on " — especially on my weak arm."
Cue Factory Gong on " — I ever had to deal with."
Cue 8 and Fly Elevator Cloth in on " — it's a losing RACE."
    Fade all to B.O. (Count of 2).
Cue 9.   When Elevator Cloth in.
    Circle Spots—Amber and Lavender/Blue Full.   Floats—All circuits to $\frac{1}{2}$.   No. 1 A.A. Bar— All Ambers and Blues Full.   No. 1 Boom—All Ambers and Blues Full.
Working-lights on.
Cue 10.   " — sure of himself for ME."
    Floats—All circuits to Full.
Working-lights out when Office Scene is set.
Cue 11.   On music pick-up after applause.
    Fade all to B.O. (Count of 6).
Fly Elevator Cloth away when Lights out.
Cue 12.   When Elevator Cloth away and desk set.
    Fade in (Count of 4): Circle Spots—6 to 19—Amber, Pink and Blue Full.   Floats—C. sections only—Amber, Pink and Blue $\frac{1}{2}$.   No. 2 Batt.—White and Blue circuits to $\frac{1}{2}$.   No. 3 Batt.— All circuits to $\frac{1}{2}$.   No. 1 Spot Bar—Office Spots Full.   No. 2 Spot Bar—Office Spots Full. No. 1 Ladder—O.P.—Single Amber lamp shining on translucency above R. office door—Full. 2 Kw. Spot on stand O.P. at $\frac{1}{2}$—shining on office backcloth.   Amber Flood at $\frac{1}{2}$—shining on back of L. office door.
Cue Phone Bell on " — had a FIGHT."
Cue 13.   " THAT'S easier said than done."
    Fade all to $\frac{1}{2}$ (Count of 4).
Cue 13a.   " — never be jealous AGAIN."
    Fade all to mark 3—Scale of 10 (Count of 4).

Cue 14.   When Hines seats Mabel on chair.
Raise all to Full (Count of 4).
Cue Phone Bell on " — Too many REJECTS."
Cue 15.   Start of " Hey There."
Fade all to ½ (Count of 4).
Cue Sound Tape when Sid replaces mouthpiece.
Cue 16, and Fly Picnic Gauze and Black Drop in.   End of " Hey There."
Fade all to B.O. (Count of 4).
Cue 17.   When Picnic Gauze and Black Drop in.
**Fade in quickly: Circle Spots—All Amber, Pink and Blue Full.   Box Pageants—All Full.
Floats—Amber, Pink and Blue circuits Full.   No. 1 Batt.—Pink and Blue circuits Full.
No. 1 A.A. Bar—All Ambers and Blues Full.   No. 1 Boom—All Ambers and Blues Full.**
Working-lights on.
Working-lights out when Picnic Scene set.
Cue 18 and Limes out when Gladys exits.
Fade all to B.O. (Count of 4).
Fly Black Drop away when lights out.
Cue 19.   Start of " Sleep Tite " music.
**Fade in quickly: No. 2 Batt.—White and Blue circuits Full.   No. 3 Batt.—Amber, Pink and
Blue circuits Full.   No. 4 Batt.—Pink and Blue circuits Full.   No. 5 Batt.—Pink and Blue
circuits Full.   No. 2 A.A. Bar—All Ambers and Blues Full.   No. 3 Pageant Bar—All Ambers
and Blues Full.   No. 1 Ladder—All Ambers and Blues Full.   No. 2 Ladder—All Ambers and
Blues Full.   1-2 Kw. Spot on stand P. side Full—Shining across L. table.   1-2 Kw. Spot on
stand O.P. Full—Shining across R. table.   Ground row—All circuits Full.**
Fly Picnic Gauze away start of " Sleep Tite " vocal.
Follow on Cue when Picnic Gauze away.
**Circle Spots—Amber and Lavender/Blue Full.   Box Pageants—All Full.   Floats—Amber,
Pink and Blue circuits Full.   No. 1 Batt.—All Amber, Pink and Blue circuits Full.   No. 1
Boom—All Ambers and Blues Full.   No. 1 A.A. Bar—All Ambers and Blues Full.**
Cue Knife throws (Four) in Picnic Scene.
Cue 23.   Start of " Once a Year Day."
Circle Spots—Centre 8 lamps (Autos)—Change to Pale Lemon.
Cue 24 and Limes Snap out when 3 Solo dancers pop up.
D.B.O.
Fly Picnic Gauze and Black Drop in when lights out.
Cue 25 when Picnic Gauze and Black Drop in.
**Fade in quickly: Circle Spots—All Blues to Full.   Floats—Blue circuit Full.   No. 1 Batt.—
Blue circuits Full.   No. 1 A.A. Bar—All Blues Full.   No. 1 Boom—All Blues Full.**
Working-lights on.
Working-lights out when Kitchen Scene set.
Cue 26 and Limes out when Mae pulls Prez off L.
Fade all to B.O. (Count of 4).
Fly Picnic Gauze and Black Drop away when lights out.
Cue 27 and Train effect when Picnic Gauze 12' high.
**Fade in (Count of 4): No. 3 Batt.—Blue circuit Full.   No. 4 Batt.—Blue circuits Full.   No. 5
Batt.—Blue circuits Full.   Signal Lights to mark 2.   Follow on with (Count of 4): Circle
Spots—Centre 8 Lamps (Autos)—Amber and Lavender/Blue Full.   No. 1 Spot Bar—Kitchen
Spots Full.   No. 2 Spot Bar—Kitchen Spot Full.   Strips below windows Full.   Baby Spot
on stand O.P. Full—Shining on back of House Piece Panel in O.P. Portal.**
Cue Train effect on " Come around any time, SID."
Cue 28.   Start of " Small Talk."
Fade all except Battens and Signal Lights to ½ (Count of 4).
Cue 29.   Tacit: " And that TAKES no talk at all."
Raise all except Battens and Signal Lights to Full (Count of 4).
Cue 30 when Babe and Sid nearly sit in chair.
**Fade all except Battens and Signal Lights to B.O.   Follow on with: Fade all Battens and
Signal Lights to B.O.**
Fly Elevator Cloth in when Truck U.S. and lights out.
Cue 30a.   When Elevator Cloth in.
**Fade in quickly: Circle Spots—Lavender/Blue Full.   Floats—Amber, Pink and Blue circuits
Full.   No. 1 A.A. Bar—All Ambers and Blues Full.   No. 1 Boom—All Ambers and Blues
Full.**
Working-lights on.
Cue 30b.   Start of " Once was a Man."
Fade all to ½ (Count of 4).
Working-lights out when Factory Scene set.
Cue 30c when Sid carries Babe off L.
Fade all quickly to B.O.

Fly Elevator Cloth away when lights out.
Cue 33 when Elevator Cloth away.
    **Fade in quickly: Circle Spots—Amber and Lavender/Blue Full. Box Pageants—All Full.
Floats—Amber, Pink and Blue circuits Full. No. 1 Batt.—Amber, Pink and Blue circuits
Full. No. 2 Batt.—Blue circuits Full. No. 3 Batt.—Blue circuits Full. No. 4 Batt.—Pink
and Blue circuits Full. No. 5 Batt.—Pink and Blue circuits Full. No. 1 A.A. Bar—All
Ambers and Blues Full. No. 2 A.A. Bar—All Ambers and Blues Full. No. 3 Pageant Bar—
All Ambers and Blues Full. No. 1 Boom—All Ambers and Blues Full. No. 1 Ladder—All
Ambers and Blues Full. No. 2 Ladder—All Ambers and Blues Full. Sewing machine
pendants Full. Ground rows—All circuits Full. 1-2 Kw. Spot on stand O.P. Full—Shining
through R. window. 1-2 Kw. Spot on stand P. Full—Shining across bench.**
Cue Factory Gong on " Attaboy, this is it."
Cue Crash effect when Babe jams machinery.
Cue 35 on " BETTER forget her."
    Fade all to ¾ (Count of 4).
Cue House Tabs in on " — and out the OTHER."
Verbal Cue when House Tabs in—House lights on.

INTERVAL

Check the following:—
    Eagle Hall Flat in. Grey Drop in. Panels clear.
Pre-set Act II. Scene 1. Eagle Hall.
    **No. 2 Batt.—Blue circuit Full. No. 1 A.A. Bar—Ambers and Blues ½. No. 1 Boom—
Ambers and Blues ½.**
1 min. before Entr'acte.
    Send M.D. in.
Star: of Entr'acte.
    **Ring 3 Bar Bells. Nos. 1 and 2 Batt. Pilots off. Verbal Cue to Elecs.: Circle Spots—3 C.
Lamps Blue ½. 2 C. Lamps Lavender ½. Floats—Amber, Pink and Blue ½. Centre section
only.**
Verbal Cue end of " Hey There " in Entr'acte—House lights out.
Cue House Tabs away at end of Entr'acte applause.
Cue 1a and Fly Eagle Flat away on " — that's what we're DOING."
    **Count of 3, Cross Fade to: Circle Spots—Blues Full. Floats—Blue circuit Full. No. 1 Boom
—2 top Amber lamps each side only, Full.**
Cue 1b on 2nd " But that don't do no GOOD."
    Fade all to B.O. (Count of 3).
Working-lights out when Kitchen Scene set.
Cue 1c. On MUSIC pick-up after Clap section.
    **Fade in (Count of 3): Circle Spots—B. es Full. Floats—Blue circuit Full. No. 1 A.A. Bar—
Blues Full.**
Cue 1d on SCREAM and slide.
    **Fade in quickly: Circle Spots—Ambers and Pinks to ½. Box Pageants—All to ½. Floats—
Amber, Pink and Blue circuits to ½. No. 1 Boom—Ambers and Blues to ½. No. 1 A.A. Bar—
Ambers to ½.**
Cue 2. As PREZ exits D.R.
    Fade all to B.O. (Count of 3).
Fly Grey Drop away when Lights out.
Cue 3 when Kitchen Truck in position.
    **Fade in (Count of 3): No. 3 Batt.—Blue circuit Full. No. 4 Batt.—Blue circuit Full. No. 5
Batt.—Blue circuit Full. Signal Lights to mark 2. Follow on (Count of 3): Circle Spots—
C. 8 Lamps—Amber and Lavender/Blue Full. No. 1 Spot Bar—Kitchen Spots Full. No. 2
Spot Bar—Kitchen Spot Full. Strips below windows Full. Baby Spot on stand O.P. Full—
Shining on back of House Piece Panel in O.P. Portal.**
Cue Limes to pick up 3 Steam Heaters if applause long enough.
Cue Phone Bell on " — that's CONSTRUCTIVE."
Cue Train effect on " — Single ones, I HOPE."
Cue 3a on " Pan American ISSUES."
    Fade all except Battens and Signal Lights to out (Count of 6).
Cue Lime on Babe when she comes through L. Panel.
Cue 4. " — are you too much in LOVE."
    Fade all to B.O. (Count of 4).
Cue Lime out on tacit phrase—" Is it all going IN."
Fly Elevator Cloth in when Truck U.S.
Cue 5. When Elevator Cloth in and last chord of music.
    **Fade in quickly: Circle Spots—All Lavender and Blue Full. Floats—All circuits Full. No. 1
Boom—All Ambers and Blues Full. No. 1 A.A. Bar—All Ambers and Blues Full.**

Working-lights on.

Working-lights out when Office Scene is set.

Cue 6 *and Limes Snap out when Hines raises hat.*

    D.B.O.

Fly Elevator Cloth away when lights out.

Cue 7. *When Elevator Cloth away and desk set.*

    Fade in quickly: Circle Spots—6, 7, 17, 18, 19—Amber and Lavender/Blue Full. 8 to 16—White Full. Floats—All circuits to ½. No. 2 Batt.—White and Blue circuits Full. No. 3 Batt.—Amber, Pink and Blue circuits Full. White circuit to ½. No. 1 Spot Bar—Office Spots Full. No. 2 Spot Bar—Office Spots Full. No. 1 Ladder—O.P. side—Single Amber lamp shining on translucency above R. office door—Full. 1-2 Kw. Spot on stand O.P. at ½—Shining on office backcloth. 1 Amber Flood on stand at ½—Shining on back of L. office door.

Cue 8. *" I know a wonderful JOINT."*

    Fade all to B.O. (Count of 4).

Traveller close medium pace and Fly Black Drop in when Sid moves D.S.

Cue 9. *When Traveller nearly closed.*

    Fade in (Count of 4): No. 1 Boom—Ambers and Blues Full.

Working-lights on.

Cue 9a *and Traveller open slow. " — but not my KEY."*

    Fade in (Count of 6): Circle Spots—Blues to ½. Floats—Amber circuit to ½. No. 1 Batt.—Amber and Blue circuits to ½.

Working-lights out when Hideaway is set.

Cue 10 *and Limes Snap out on " Joe sent US."*

    D.B.O. And switch on: Sign Cloth—" Hernando's Hideaway," " Chop Suey," Red arrows.

Cue 11 *and Fly Black Drop away on music change.*

    Switch off: " Hernando's Hideaway " and " Chop Suey." Follow on when Cloth going away—Switch off Red arrows.

Cue 12. *" Then strike a match and you will KNOW."*

    Snap in: Circle Spots—All Amber and Lavender/Blue to ½. Floats—Blue circuit to ½. No. 2 Batt.—Blue circuit to ¾. No. 4 Batt.—Blue circuit to Full. No. 5 Batt.—Blue circuit to Full. No. 1 A.A. Bar—1 Amber Lamp extreme R. to mark 2. No. 2 A.A. Bar—Blues to ½. No. 1 Boom—Ambers and Blues to ½. Hanging Lanterns to mark 4. 3 Neon Signs U.S. of windows to ½. Juke Box light to ½.

Cue 13. *After applause for number.*

    Fade all Circle Spots out (Count of 3).

Cue 14. *" I CAN see what marriage with Gladys — "*

    Fade all to B.O. (Count of 4).

Fly Lantern Cloth away when lights out.

Cue 15. *When Hideaway trucks half open.*

    Fade in (Count of 4): Circle Spots—C. 8 Lamps—Pale Lemon—Full. Floats—Blue circuit Full. No. 2 Batt.—Blue circuit Full. No. 3 Batt.—Blue circuit Full. No. 4 Batt.—White and Blue circuits Full. No. 6 Batt.—Amber circuit to mark 7. No. 2 Spot Bar—4 Spots Full.

Cue Moose eyes when Gladys rises from floor.

Cue Moose eyes as Gladys sprays bed.

Cue Moose eyes when Frenchman goes to dive on Gladys.

Cue Moose eyes when Gladys kisses Wrestler.

Cue 20 *and Fly Black Drop in on COUNT* 18 *of music for boys out of cupboard.*

    Cross Fade all in Cue 15 to (Count of 6): Circle Spots—Blue lamps to Full. Floats—Amber circuit to Full. No. 1 Batt.—Blue circuit to Full.

Working-lights on.

Working-lights out when Office Scene set.

Cue 21 *and Limes Snap out when Angel exits L.*

    D.B.O.

Fly Black Drop away when lights out.

Cue 22. *When Black Drop away.*

    Fade in quickly: Circle Spots—6, 7, 17, 18, 19—Amber and Lavender/Blue Full. 8 to 16—White Full. Floats—All circuits to ½. No. 2 Batt.—White and Blue circuits Full. No. 3 Batt.—Amber, Pink and Blue circuits Full. White circuit to ½. No. 1 Spot Bar—Office Spots Full. No. 2 Spot Bar—Office Spots Full. No. 1 Ladder—O.P. side—Single Amber lamp shining on translucency above R. office door—Full. 1-2 Kw. Spot on stand O.P. at ½—Shining on office backcloth. 1 Amber Flood on stand at ½—Shining on back of L. office door.

Cue 23. *" I'll break IT."*

    Fade in (Count of 4): Circle Spots—22 and 23—Full. Box Pageants—1 lamp O.P. to Full.

Cue 3 *Knife effects on cues.*

Cue 24 *and Limes Snap out. " — sit down and talk to ME."*

    D.B.O.

Close Traveller fast and Fly lack Drop in when lights out.

Cue 25.   When Traveller nearly closed.

Fade in (Count of 4): Circle Spots—All Amber and Lavender/Blue Full.   Box Pageants— All Full.   Floats—All circuits Full.   No. 1 Boom—All Ambers and Blues Full.   No. 1 A.A. Bar—All Ambers Full.

Working-lights on.

Working-lights out when Finale set.

Fly Black Drop away on " They'll never LAST."

Cue 26 and Traveller Open fast on " — dress for the OCCASION."

Fade in quickly: No. 1 A.A. Bar—All Blues Full.   Hanging Lanterns to Full.   3 Neon Signs U.S. of windows to Full.   Change 8 C. Circle Spots to Pale Lemon.

House Tabs in on " same as the PAJAMA game."

House Tabs up on COUNT 4 of " Seven-and-a-half Cents " intro.

House Tabs in on 2nd " — living like a KING."

House Tabs for ad lib calls.

Verbal Cue for House-lights with House Tabs raised for Anthem.

PROPERTY PLOT

Act I.   Scene 1.   *Swatch Traveller.   Prologue.*
Personal: Large stop-watch and ribbon—Hines.
Act I.   Scene 2.   *Factory.*
Pre-set: From C. stage extending to off L., factory bench, with following articles on it: 12
               sewing machines—6 each side, staggered to prevent masking. 38 spools of thread
               on spindles, placed beside each machine and on rack above machines. Dressing
               of pieces of different coloured materials.
               (Note: There are 5 large pieces of cloth draped along the D.S. edge of the bench
               to cover all the lower part of the bench, in the following order, reading from C. stage
               to off L.—Bright Red; Bright Yellow; Aquamarine; Bright Orange; Bright Blue.
               The rest of the bench is littered with other varying sizes and colours of cloth.)
               6 high stools U.S. of the bench. 6 bentwood chairs D.S. of the bench.
               (Note: These stools and chairs are also staggered to prevent masking—one to each
               machine.)
               Cable housing and outlet under U.R. machine.
               (Note: This cable is connected to a long cable which hangs from the flys.)
               Piece of loose cable under No. 9 machine. Medium-sized carton containing pieces
               of material at R. end of bench. 2 large cartons and one large bolt of material,
               draped with pieces of material, set U.S.C. against back wall. 3 brown paper
               patterns stuck on back wall—R. of R. window. 4 bolts of material and 5 rolls of
               materialslying on and leaning against window seat S.R. 3 cartons of material by
               window s eat S.R. Green curtain over lower parts of 3 U.S. windows.
From S/R: 1 Pushwagon, with 3 piles of pajama boxes on bottom shelf.
               (Note: These boxes are all labelled " Sleep Tite.")
               4 rolls of material—Dancing boys. 4 cartons, tied together—Dancing boy. 2 small
               cartons with scraps of material—Dancing boy. 2 bundles of brown-paper patterns—
               Singing boy. 1 gong—offstage effect.
From S/L: 1 tool box containing—1 pair of pliers, 1 screwdriver, 1 roll of insulating tape, 1 coil
               of wire, 1 pin connector.
               (Note: The 2nd Helper carries this on.)
               1 pajama rack with 20 pairs of pajamas hanging on it—2 Dancing boys. 1 pair of
               pajamas—Singing boy. 1 clip-board and pencil—Singing boy. 4 rolls of material—
               Dancing boy. 6 small boxes tied together—Dancing boy. 4 medium-sized cartons
               with material—Dancing boy.
Act I.   Scene 3.   *The Hallway (Elevator).*
From S/R: 1 pushwagon, with top clear and bottom shelf containing pajama boxes—2 Singing
               girls.
Personal: 1 apple—Babe.
Act I.   Scene 4.   *The Office.*
Pre-set: 1 large filing cabinet D.L. 1 wire paper tray on top of cabinet, containing loose
               letters. 1 large old-fashioned desk U.S. of cabinet, with following articles on it—
               1 old-fashioned typewriter (paper in it); 1 upright telephone; 1 wire letter tray
               (loose letters in it); Dressing, papers, etc., in pigeon-holes; Electric fan on shelf
               above desk. (Not practical.) Pile of ledgers on shelf above desk. 1 waste-paper
               basket D.S. of desk (crumpled papers in it). 1 bentwood chair at desk. 1 calendar
               on wall U.S. of desk. 1 broken window pole hanging on clip on back wall, between
               the two windows. 2 green roller blinds on windows on back wall (Practical).
               1 Hall tree U.S.R., with hat and coat on it. 1 flat-topped desk set stage R., with
               following articles on it—1 Dictaphone (R. end of desk); 1 modern telephone (L. end
               of desk); 1 Steno pad; 1 large sheet of blotting paper; 1 flat inkwell; 2 pencils; 6 bill-
               heads. 1 swivel office chair U.S. of desk. 1 bentwood chair L. end of desk.
From S/R: 1 telephone bell effect (Practical).
From S/L: Locked ledger—Gladys.
Personal: Key on chair—Gladys. Picnic tickets—Poopsie. Purse with loose change—Mabel.
Act I.   Scene 5.   *Picnic Crossover.*
From S/L: 1 baseball bat—Dancing boy. 1 soft ball—Dancing boy. 2 baseball gloves—Singing
               and Dancing boys. 2 picnic baskets—Girls. 1 inner tube—Girl. 4 rubber beach
               animals—Girls. 2 beach bags—Boys. 1 rubber beach ball—Girl. 1 small beer
               keg—2 Singing boys. 1 spigot—Dancing girl. 1 suitcase—Prez.
               (Note: This case must be strong enough to allow Prez to sit on it.)
Act I.   Scene 6.   *Picnic.*
Pre-set: 1 wooden trestle table set S.L., with following articles on it—Dinner bell—Poopsie;
               Beer keg on trestles (L. end of table); Numerous beer bottles, beer cans, beer mugs
               and paper cups. 1 wooden stool and 3 canvas stools D.S. of table. 1 wooden
               bench U.S. of table. 1 wooden trestle table set U.S.R., with following articles on

it—Numerous beer bottles, beer mugs, beer cans and paper cups. 4 canvas stools U.S. of table. 1 wooden bench D.S. of table. Knife board on marks S.R. 1 small table with 9 knives on it, set U.S. of knife board. 4 knives in plungers in board. 2 canvas stools in front of knife board. Folded blanket in R. portal.

From S/R: 1 portable radio—Dancing boy. 1 small box camera—Dancing boy.
Personal: 1 cut apple—Babe.

Act I. Scene 7. Picnic Crossover.
From S/R: 1 beer bottle—Charlie. 1 beer bottle—Dancing boy. 2 rubber beach animals—Girls.

Act I. Scene 8. Kitchen.
Pre-set: 1 coat rack on wall D.S.L.—2 hooks on it. 1 wooden coat hanger on rack. 1 rug L.C. 1 Morris chair on rug L.C. 1 small table U.S. of Morris chair—3 magazines on it. 1 large ice-box U.S.L., with following articles in it—9 capped beer bottles; 2 cans of beer; 1 butter dish; Half a loaf of bread, wrapped in transparent bag; Bowl of eggs; 3 milk bottles. 1 Geranium plant on cupboard U.S.L. 2 bottle openers on cupboard U.S.L. Plates in dish rack at sink. Soap in soap dish at sink. 4 kitchen canisters on draining board. 2 kitchen towels in drawer L. of door U.S.C. Metal lunch box on draining board—handle upwards. 1 calendar on wall U.S.R. 3 packets of soap powders and scourers on cupboard U.R. 2 cups and saucers on cupboard U.R. 1 kettle on 3-burner gas stove U.R. 1 pot-holder on hook R. of door U.C. 1 coffee pot on cupboard U.R. 1 frying pan and 2 saucepans on cupboard D.S.R. 1 upright telephone on D.S. end of cupboard D.S.R. 1 bread tin on cupboard S.R. 3 beer steins on cupboard S.R. 2 glasses on cupboard S.R. 1 cream-painted kitchen table, set R.C. 2 cream-painted kitchen chairs, set with one at L. end and one at R. end of table. 1 yellowish checked table-cloth on kitchen table. 1 cup and saucer on kitchen table. 1 folded newspaper on kitchen table. Matching sets of greenish patterned curtains and pelmets at the following points—Over door alcove in stage L. panel; Covering alcove under sink; Over window section of door U.S.C.; Curtains and pelmets at 3 windows on kitchen walls.

From S/L: 1 stamp album—Pop.
(Note: This album has stamps stuck on the first two pages.)
Personal: 1 petrified bat—Pop.
(Note: Strike Babe's dress and Sid's sports coat from rack D.L., and Babe's belt from S.R. cupboard at end of scene.)

Act I. Scene 9. The Hallway (Elevator).
NO PROPS.

Act I. Scene 10. The Factory.
Pre-set: Same setting as in Act I. Scene 2, plus—1 pair of red pajamas on cartons S.R. Flash effect under No. 9 machine (Practical).
(Note: The asbestos box which contains the flash effect, and the two switches which Sid operates the flash with are permanent fixtures.)
From S/R: 1 roll of material—Dancing boy. 3 small boxes—Dancing boy. 1 length of red and white striped material—Singing girl.
From S/L: 1 pair of blue pajamas—Singing girl. 1 clipboard and pencil—Singing boy. Switch and screwdriver—Charlie. 3 rolls of material—Dancing boy. 3 cartons—Dancing boy.

INTERVAL

Act II. Scene 1. Eagle Hall.
Pre-set: On Eagle Hall flat—1 Union banner; 2 Union leaders' photographs (Blow-ups).
Act II. Scene 2. Kitchen.
Pre-set: Same as in Act I. Scene 8, plus—5 capped beer bottles on cupboard U.L.; 3 more kitchen chairs at table S.R.—One set D.S. of table, and two set U.S. of table. On kitchen table S.R. the following articles—4 uncapped beer bottles; 3 beer steins; 1 whisky bottle; 1 highball glass; 1 bottle opener; 1 cup, saucer and spoon.
From S/L: 1 metal lunch box—Pop. 1 stamp album—Pop.
Personal: Letter in envelope—Prez.
Act II. Scene 3. Tick Tock Scene.
From S/L: Cardboard box containing pair of pajamas—Salesman.
Act II. Scene 4. Office.
Pre-set: Same as Act I. Scene 4, except—Chair L. of desk R. is now set against back wall, L. of U.L. window. Newspaper on desk S.L.
From S/R: Pair of pajamas in box—Salesman.
(Note: The trousers of these pajamas are weighted so that they fall down easily when required in the scene.)
From S/L: Locked ledger—Gladys.

Act II.   Scene 4a.   Intermediate Scene—Hernando's Crossover.
Personal: Prop cigar, straw hat, castanets—" Steam-Heat " boy.
Act II.   Scene 5.   Hernando's Hideaway.
Pre-set: Juke Box D.S.L. (Practical light in it).   3-tread steps behind Juke Box.
(Note: One of the Dancing boys climbs from these steps to the top of the Juke Box during the scene.   When he comes off the Juke Box the steps are pulled off L.)
4 red and white checked tablecloths on tables in booths L. and R.   4 pairs of brownish net curtains covering booths L. and R.   6 strings of property fruit and gourds— dressing for tops of booths L. and R.   Sprays of green leaves to dress trellis work at D.S.C. part of booths L. and R.   1 round table C. stage, with padded top.   1 red and white checked table cloth on table C.   2 shot glasses on table C.   2 single chairs set L. and R. of C. table.   1 round table D.S.R.   1 red and white checked tablecloth on table D.S.R.   3 single chairs, set L. and R. and U.S. of table D.S.R.   4 highball glasses on table D.S.R.   Folding screen set U.S. of table D.S.R.   5 ashtrays—One to each booth table, and one on table D.S.R.
(Note: The Fire Regulations for this scene require that a Fireman should stand by at one side of the stage, and a Property man at the other side.   Each man should have available a fire-bucket filled with water for an emergency.)
From S/R: Numerous special matches—Boys and girls.   Fire bucket filled with water.
From S/L: Numerous special matches—Boys and girls.   Fire bucket filled with water.   1 tray with 3 shot glasses—Waiter.   1 knife—Hines.
Personal: Paper money—Sid.
Act II.   Scene 5a.   Jealousy Ballet.
Pre-set: In wardrobe S.L.—1 small cushion; 1 trilby hat; 1 briefcase; 1 negligee; 1 pair of black court shoes.
(Note: The negligee and the court shoes are set in the wardrobe by Glady's dresser.)
1 black cloak—Dressing for interior.   On bed S.R.—1 purple silk bed spread; 1 lace bed spread; 1 purple silk-covered bolster; 2 purple silk-covered pillows; 5 small cushions.
(Note: These cushions have a purple silk cover over which there is a lace cover with a rose sewn on it.)
1 French doll.   1 atomiser.   Moosehead on French flat U.S.C., above door.
(Note: This Moosehead has large red eyes which light up during the scene Operated on Cue from Prompt Corner.)
From S/R: 1 pail—Gladys.   1 scrubbing brush—Gladys.   1 hair net with curlers sewn on it— Gladys.   1 frumpy bathrobe—Gladys.
Intermediate Scene—Black Drop—" Strip " Ballet.
From S/R: 1 very large knife—Hines.
Act II.   Scene 6.   Office.
Pre-set: Same as Act I. Scene 4, plus—3 knives in plungers in wall marks S.L.; Unlocked ledger on desk S.R.; 3 coffee cartons on desk S.R.; 2 milk cartons on desk S.R.
From S/R: 1 small pair of steps—Charlie.   1 knife—Hines.
Personal: Ledger key on chain—Sid.
Act II.   Scene 7.   Seven-and a-Half Cents.
Personal: Union sash—Prez.   Pad and pencil—Prez.
Finale.
Pre-set: Booths on new marks.   Pair of black draw curtains set C.
(Note: These curtains are on an inset piece set between the D.S. ends of the booths. The strings to open and close them on Cue hang in the D.R. booth where one of the Singing boys operates them.)
Additional string of fruit and gourds hanging above C. curtains.   Set of black drapes in alcove U.S. of C. curtains for masking purposes.   1 round table and 3 chairs set U.R.   1 red and white checked tablecloth on table U.R.   1 round table and 4 chairs set U.L.   1 red and white checked tablecloth on table U.L.   22 pairs of children's pajamas draped across stage above booths.
(Note: These pajamas are separately coloured red, white and blue.)
From S/R: Long chain with snap wrist fastener—Gladys and Hines.

WARDROBE PLOT

BABE WILLIAMS

Act I. Scene 2. Factory Scene.
1 green check skirt with fitted white petticoat. 1 white pleated blouse with high collar.
1 pair black patent court shoes. 1 pair tan fish-net stockings. 1 blue smock, edged white.
Act I. Scene 3. Elevator Scene.
Repeat Act I, Scene 2, with the exception of—Blue smock, edged white.
Act I. Scene 4. Office Scene.
Repeat Act I, Scene 3.
Act I. Scene 6. Picnic Scene.
1 green silk dress with fitted white petticoat. 1 pair green satin court shoes. 1 pair tan
fish-net stockings.
Act I. Scene 8. Kitchen Scene.
1 black and white check dress with zipper down front of dress. 1 black patent leather belt.
1 black silk and lace slip. Repeat stockings and patent court shoes, Act I, Scene 2.
Act I. Scene 9. Elevator Scene.
1 dark blue wrap-over overall. Repeat slip, stockings and shoes, Act I, Scene 8.
Act I. Scene 10. Factory Scene.
Repeat Act I, Scene 9, with the addition of—Blue smock, edged white, Act I, Scene 2.
Act II. Scene 2. Kitchen Scene.
1 red figured peasant skirt with fitted white petticoat. 1 white peasant blouse with inter-
woven red velvet ribbon round neck. Repeat stockings, shoes and belt, Act I, Scene 8.
Act II. Scene 5. Hernando's Hideaway.
1 purple silk dress with fitted white petticoat. Repeat stockings and shoes Act II, Scene 2.
Act II. Scene 6. Office Scene.
1 plain green skirt. 1 pink blouse. Repeat stockings, shoes and belt, Act II, Scene 2.
Act II. Scene 7. Seven-and-a-half Cents.
Repeat Act II, Scene 6.
Act II. Scene 7. Finale.
1 shantung pajama jacket with large trimmed red hearts. 1 pair shantung knickers.
Repeat stockings and shoes, Act II, Scene 6.

GLADYS

Act I. Scene 2. Factory Scene.
1 blue dress with white spots with white trimming round neck, sleeves and waist—Polo style
neck-line—Fitted white petticoat in dress. 1 pair white court shoes.
Act I. Scene 4. Office Scene.
Repeat Act I, Scene 2.
Act I. Scene 5. Picnic Crossover.
1 pair black and white striped trousers. 1 black jersey top. 1 red silk scarf. 1 pair black
court shoes.
Act I. Scene 6. Picnic Scene.
1 yellow and black flowered dress. 1 pair green flat-heeled shoes. 1 pair white knickers.
Act I. Scene 10. Factory Scene.
1 yellow and white dress with fitted petticoat. Repeat shoes, Act I, Scene 2.
Act II. Scene 1. Eagle Hall (Steam Heat).
1 black suit (jacket and trousers). 1 white shirt. 1 black bowler hat. 1 pair flat black
shoes. 1 pair white socks. 1 red bow tie.
Act II. Scene 4. Office Scene.
1 pair black fish-net stockings. 1 pair black lace knickers. 1 black lace corselette. 1 pair
black court shoes. 1 dress with plain mauve top and brown and white striped skirt.
Intermediate Scene. Hernando's Crossover.
Repeat Act II, Scene 4.
Act II. Scene 5. Hernando's Hideaway.
1 black and red spotted silk dress. Repeat shoes, stockings, knickers and corselette, Act II,
Scene 4.
Act II. Scene 5a. Jealousy Ballet.
1 blue dressing gown in tattered condition. 1 pair brown velvet slippers. 1 hair-net with
fitted curlers on it. Repeat shoes, stockings, knickers and corselette, Act II, Scene 5. 1 pink
and black lace negligee.
Intermediate Scene. Strip Ballet.
Repeat Act II, Scene 5a.
Act II. Scene 6. Office Scene.
Repeat Act II, Scene 4.

Act II.   Scene 7.   Finale.
1 pair black and white striped pajamas with large red heart sewn on left breast of jacket—the jacket is horizontally striped and the trousers are vertically striped.   Repeat shoes, Act II, Scene 6.

MABEL

Act I.   Scene 2.   Factory Scene.
1 green tweed costume.   1 white blouse.   1 pair black walking shoes.   1 pair nylon stockings. 1 red sloppy tie with brooch fastener.
Act I.   Scene 4.   Office Scene.
Repeat Act I, Scene 2.
Act I.   Scene 6.   Picnic Scene.
1 yellow print dress.   1 pair coloured beach sandals.   1 yellow straw hat, trimmed red poppy.   1 yellow straw basket.   1 basket-style handbag.   1 pair green gloves.   Repeat stockings, Act I, Scene 4.
Act I.   Scene 7.   Picnic Crossover.
Repeat Act I, Scene 6, with the exception of yellow straw basket.
Act I.   Scene 10.   Factory Scene.
Repeat Act I, Scene 4.
Act II.   Scene 4.   Office Scene.
1 grey serge dress with white cuffs and collar.   1 pair brown walking shoes.   Repeat stockings, Act I, Scene 4.
Intermediate Scene.   Strip Ballet.
1 white nylon angel costume with hem, cuffs and collar trimmed in white swansdown. 1 pair swansdown wings.   1 pair blue flat shoes.   1 silver halo.
Act II.   Scene 7.   Finale.
1 red pajama suit, yellow spotted.   Hat, sandals and hand-bag, Act I, Scene 6.

MAE

Act I.   Scene 2.   Factory Scene.
1 grey tweed costume skirt.   1 white shirt blouse.   1 pair black court shoes.   1 pair nylon stockings.   1 flowered overall coat.
Act I.   Scene 3.   Elevator Scene.
Repeat as Act I, Scene 2.
Act I.   Scene 5.   Picnic Crossover.
1 pair brown trousers.   1 yellow painted blouse —jacket style.   1 pair brown court shoes. 1 red chiffon handkerchief.
Act I.   Scene 6.   Picnic Scene.
Repeat as Act I, Scene 5.
Act I.   Scene 7.   Picnic Crossover.
Repeat as Act I, Scene 6.
Act I.   Scene 9.   Elevator Scene.
Repeat as Act I, Scene 3.
Act I.   Scene 10.   Factory Scene.
Repeat as Act I, Scene 9.
Act II.   Scene 2.   Kitchen Scene.
Repeat as Act I, Scene 3—with the exception of the overall coat and with the addition of 1 grey tweed costume jacket.
Act II.   Scene 5.   Hernando's Hideaway.
1 purple figured dress.   1 white nylon slip.   Repeat black shoes and stockings as Act II, Scene 2.
Act II.   Scene 7.   Seven-and-a-Half Cents.
Repeat as Act II, Scene 2.
Act II.   Scene 7.   Finale.
1 white nightdress.   Repeat black shoes and stockings as Act II, Scene 5.

BRENDA

Act I.   Scene 2.   Factory Scene.
1 tweed skirt.   1 yellow blouse.   1 black belt.   1 blue and white striped overall.   1 pair black court shoes.   1 pair nylon stockings.
Act I.   Scene 3.   Elevator Scene.
Repeat as Act I, Scene 2.
Act I.   Scene 5.   Picnic Crossover.
1 pair purple trousers.   1 mauve blouse.   1 black belt.   1 pair beach sandals.
Act I.   Scene 6.   Picnic Scene.
Repeat as Act I, Scene 5.
Act I.   Scene 9.   Elevator Scene.
Repeat as Act I, Scene 2.

Act I. Scene 10. Factory Scene.
Repeat as Act I, Scene 2, with the exception of blue and white striped overall.
Act II. Scene 2. Kitchen Scene.
1 orange skirt. 1 brown painted peasant blouse. Repeat black shoes and stockings, Act I, Scene 2.
Act II. Scene 7. Seven-and-a-Half Cents.
Repeat as Act I, Scene 10.
Act II. Scene 7. Finale.
1 pair pajamas, jacket red, trousers and sash white with red spots. Repeat black shoes and stockings, Act I, Scene 2.

POOPSIE

Act I. Scene 2. Factory Scene.
1 blue skirt. 1 yellow blouse. 1 blue printed pinafore. 1 pair black court shoes. 1 pair nylon stockings.
Act I. Scene 3. Elevator Scene.
Repeat as Act I, Scene 2.
Act I. Scene 4. Office Scene.
Repeat as Act I, Scene 2.
Act I. Scene 5. Picnic Crossover.
1 blue elastic swim-suit. 1 pair black court shoes.
Act I. Scene 6. Picnic Scene.
Repeat as Act I, Scene 5.
Act I. Scene 9. Elevator Scene.
Repeat as Act I, Scene 2.
Act I. Scene 10. Factory Scene.
Repeat as Act I, Scene 2, except blue printed pinafore.
Act II. Scene 5. Hernando's Hideaway.
1 royal blue and black dress. Repeat shoes and stockings as Act I, Scene 2.
Act II. Scene 7. Seven-and-a-Half Cents.
1 red dress trimmed white on collar. 1 white petticoat. 1 pair black court shoes. 1 pair nylon stockings.
Act II. Scene 7. Finale.
1 pair blue pajama trousers. 1 jersey top—blue and white horizontal stripes. Repeat shoes and stockings, Act II, Scene 7. Seven-and-a-Half Cents.

SINGING AND DANCING GIRLS

Various dresses and costumes to all Scenes plus pajamas for Finale.

SID SOROKIN

Act I. Scene 2. Factory.
1 pair brown slacks. 1 brown striped shirt. 1 pair brown socks. 1 pair brown shoes (Casuals). 1 brown leather belt.
Act I. Scene 3. Elevator Scene.
Repeat as Act I, Scene 2.
Act I. Scene 4. Office Scene.
1 cream shirt. Repeat slacks, socks, shoes and belt, Act I, Scene 2.
Act I. Scene 6. Picnic Scene.
1 pair grey slacks. 1 blue and red striped T-shirt. 1 pair brown suede shoes. Repeat socks and belt, Act I, Scene 2.
Act I. Scene 8. Kitchen Scene.
1 pair blue slacks. 1 white shirt. 1 blue tie. 1 grey sports jacket. Repeat shoes, socks and belt, Act I, Scene 2.
Act I. Scene 9. Elevator Scene.
Repeat as Act I, Scene 8, with the exception of Grey sports jacket and blue tie.
Act I. Scene 10. Factory.
Repeat as Act I, Scene 2.
Act II. Scene 2. Kitchen Scene.
1 sand coloured linen jacket. 1 dark brown shirt. Repeat slacks, socks, shoes and belt, Act I, Scene 2.
Act II. Scene 4. Office Scene.
1 dark blue suit. 1 pair black shoes. 1 pair blue socks. Repeat white shirt, Act I, Scene 8.
Act II. Scene 5. Hernando's Hideaway.
Repeat as Act II, Scene 4, plus plain blue tie.

Act II.   Scene 6.   Office Scene.
   Repeat as Act I, Scene 2.
Act II.   Scene 7.   Seven-and-a-Half Cents.
   Repeat as Act I, Scene 2.
Act II.   Scene 7.   Finale.
   1 pair shantung pajama trousers trimmed with large red hearts.   Repeat shoes and socks, Act I, Scene 2.

HINES

Act I.   Scene 1.   Prologue.
   1 green pork-pie hat.   1 grey alpaca jacket.   1 pair black trousers with white pin-spots on them.   1 pair black shoes.   1 pair white socks.   1 white shirt.   1 pair black armlets. 1 red bow tie.   1 leather belt.
Act I.   Scene 2.   Factory.
   Repeat as Act I, Scene 1.
Act I.   Scene 4.   Office Scene.
   Repeat as Act I, Scene 1.
Act I.   Scene 6.   Picnic Scene.
   1 sand coloured 2-piece linen suit.   1 white shirt.   1 check patterned cap.   1 pair brown shoes.   Repeat tie and socks, Act I, Scene 1.
Act I.   Scene 10.   Factory.
   Repeat as Act I, Scene 1.
Act II   Scene 3.   Tick Tock Scene.
   1 pair light grey trousers—the flys are fitted with a zipper, and inside the fly flap is a small snap-hook to attach the ring on the shirt sleeve.   1 white nylon shirt—there is a small ring sewn on the left cuff to attach to the snap-hook on the trousers.   1 red bow tie.   1 leather belt.   1 pair yellow flowered underpants.   Repeat jacket, shoes, socks and hat, Act I, Scene 1.
Act II.   Scene 4.   Office Scene.
   Repeat as Act II, Scene 3—except jacket.
Act II.   Scene 5.   Hernando's Hideaway.
   1 pair striped morning trousers.   1 white soft shirt with tie attached for quick change. Repeat jacket, shoes and socks as Act I, Scene 1.
Act II.   Scene 5a.   Jealousy Ballet.
   Repeat as Act II, Scene 5, with in addition—1 battered trilby hat.   1 morning suit jacket. 1 white dicky with grey stock tie and grey waistcoat attached.   1 black velvet artist's hat. 1 white and blue quilted dressing gown.   1 blonde wig.
Intermediate Scene.   Strip Scene.
   Repeat as Act II, Scene 5.
Act II.   Scene 6.   Office Scene.
   1 white shirt.   Repeat trousers, shoes, socks and tie, Act II, Scene 5.
Act II.   Scene 7.   Seven-and-a-Half Cents.
   Repeat as Act I, Scene 1.
Act II.   Scene 7.   Finale.
   1 pair black and white striped pajamas.   Jacket—thick horizontal stripes, red heart on pocket.   Trousers—thick vertical stripes.   Repeat shoes and socks, Act II, Scene 5.

PREZ

Act I.   Scene 2.   Factory.
   1 pair blue striped trousers.   1 navy blue shirt.   1 pair yellow braces.   1 pair blue socks. 1 pair black shoes.
Act I.   Scene 3.   Elevator Scene.
   Repeat as Act I, Scene 2.
Act I.   Scene 5.   Picnic Crossover.
   1 pair grey flannels.   1 coloured shirt (coat-style).   1 pair white socks.   1 straw cap— white with black horizontal stripes.   1 pair black and white sports shoes.
Act I.   Scene 6.   Picnic Scene.
   Repeat as Act I, Scene 5.
Act I.   Scene 9.   Elevator Scene.
   Repeat as Act I, Scene 2, with in addition—1 blue striped jacket to match trousers.
Act I.   Scene 10.   Factory Scene.
   Repeat as Act I, Scene 9.
Act II.   Scene 1.   Eagle Hall.
   Repeat as Act I, Scene 10, with in addition—1 white striped tie.
Act II.   Scene 2.   Kitchen Scene.
   Repeat as Act II, Scene 1.
Act II.   Scene 5.   Hernando's Hideaway.
   1 white shirt.   1 blue tie.   Repeat suit, braces, shoes and socks as Act II, Scene 2.

Act II. Scene 6. Office Scene.
Repeat as Act I, Scene 10.
Act II. Scene 7. Seven-and-a-Half Cents.
Repeat as Act II, Scene 1, with in addition—1 blue sash—" A.G.M. of A. No. 343 " printed on it.
Act II. Scene 7. Finale.
1 pair blue and black vertical striped pajamas. Repeat shoes and socks from previous scene.

HASLER

Act I. Scene 2. Factory.
1 light grey 2-piece suit. 1 white shirt. 1 grey tie. 1 pair blue socks. 1 pair black shoes.
Act I. Scene 4. Office Scene.
Repeat as Act I, Scene 2.
Act I. Scene 6. Picnic Scene.
1 cream coloured 2-piece linen suit. 1 pair brown and white shoes. Repeat tie, shoes and socks, Act I, Scene 2.
Act I. Scene 10. Factory.
Repeat as Act I, Scene 2.
Act II. Scene 4. Office Scene.
Repeat as Act I, Scene 2.
Act II. Scene 6. Office Scene.
Repeat as Act I, Scene 2.
Act II. Scene 7. Finale.
1 pair wine and grey vertical striped pajamas. Repeat shoes and socks, Act I, Scene 2.

SALESMAN

Act I. Scene 5. Picnic Crossover.
1 grey check 2-piece suit. 1 yellow check waistcoat with brass buttons. 1 cream coloured shirt. 1 red fancy bow tie. 1 white Panama hat with wine band. 1 pair brown shoes. 1 pair brown socks.
Act I. Scene 6. Picnic Scene.
Repeat as Act I, Scene 5.
Act I. Scene 7. Picnic Crossover.
Repeat as Act I, Scene 5.
Act II. Scene 3. Tick Tock Scene.
Repeat as Act I, Scene 5.
Act II. Scene 4. Office Scene.
Repeat as Act I, Scene 5.
Act II. Scene 7. Finale.
1 white night gown with red polka dots. 1 white night cap. Repeat shoes and socks, Act I, Scene 5.

POP

Act I. Scene 8. Kitchen Scene.
1 blue boiler suit and jacket. 1 grey flannel shirt. 1 red and white neckerchief. 1 blue engineer's cap. 1 pair black socks. 1 pair black shoes.
Act II. Scene 2. Kitchen Scene.
Repeat as Act I, Scene 8.
Act II. Scene 7. Finale.
1 red night gown. 1 red night cap. Repeat shoes and socks, Act I, Scene 8.

CHARLIE

Act I. Scene 2. Factory.
1 pair blue overalls. 1 red check shirt. 1 green engineer's cap. 1 pair brown socks. 1 pair black shoes.
Act I. Scene 3. Elevator Scene.
Repeat as Act I, Scene 2.
Act I. Scene 6. Picnic Scene.
1 brown 2-piece suit. 1 cream coloured shirt. 1 pair brown shoes. 1 cream coloured straw hat with gold band. Repeat socks, Act I, Scene 2.
Act I. Scene 7. Picnic Crossover.
Repeat as Act I, Scene 6.
Act I. Scene 10. Factory.
Repeat as Act I, Scene 2.
Act II. Scene 6. Office Scene.
Repeat as Act I, Scene 2.
Act II. Scene 7. Finale.
1 blue vertical striped pair of pajamas. Repeat shoes and socks, Act I, Scene 2.

DANCING BOY—"STEAM HEAT" BOY I

Act I.   Scene 2.   Factory.
  1 pair blue jeans.   1 navy shirt.   1 pair wine coloured socks.   1 pair black shoes.
Act I.   Scene 6.   Picnic Scene.
  1 pair white trousers.   1 brightly coloured floral shirt.   1 pair white socks.   1 pair white canvas shoes.
Act II.   Scene 1.   Steam Heat.
  1 black 2-piece suit.   1 black bowler hat.   1 white shirt.   1 wine coloured bow tie.   Repeat shoes and socks, Act I, Scene 2.
Act II.   Scene 4a.   Hernando's Crossover.
  1 dark grey 2-piece lounge suit.   1 gold coloured bow tie.   Repeat shirt, shoes and socks, Act II, Scene 1.
Act II.   Scene 5.   Hernando's Hideaway.
  Repeat as Act II, Scene 4a.
Act II.   Scene 7.   Seven-and-a-Half Cents.
  Repeat as Act I, Scene 2.
Act II.   Scene 7.   Finale.
  1 pair light blue pajamas.   Repeat shoes and socks, Act I, Scene 2.

DANCING BOY—"STEAM-HEAT" BOY II

Act I.   Scene 2.   Factory.
  1 pair blue jeans.   1 navy blue and yellow check shirt.   1 pair white socks.   1 pair black shoes.
Act I.   Scene 5.   Picnic Crossover.
  1 wine and white multi-coloured shirt.   1 pair white shoes.   Repeat socks and jeans, Act I, Scene 2.
Act I.   Scene 6.   Picnic Scene.
  Repeat as Act I, Scene 5.
Act II.   Scene 1.   Steam Heat.
  1 black 2-piece suit.   1 black bowler hat.   1 wine coloured bow tie.   Repeat shoes and socks, Act I, Scene 2.
Act II.   Scene 4a.   Hernando's Crossover.
  1 dark grey pin-head 2-piece suit.   1 black silk top hat.   1 long black opera cloak lined with red satin.   1 grey bow tie.   Repeat shoes and socks, Act I, Scene 2.
Act II.   Scene 5a.   Jealousy Ballet.
  1 red and gold page-boy suit.   Repeat shoes and socks, Act I, Scene 2.
Intermediate Scene.   Srip Ballet.
  Repeat as Act II, Scene 5a.
Act II.   Scene 7.   Seven-and-a-Half Cents.
  Repeat as Act I, Scene 2.
Act II.   Scene 7.   Finale.
  1 pair light blue pajamas.   Repeat shoes and socks Act I, Scene 2.

FIRST HELPER

Act I.   Scene 2.   Factory.
  1 pair blue jeans.   1 grey shirt.   1 pair fancy socks.   1 pair black shoes.
Act I.   Scene 5.   Picnic Crossover.
  1 2-piece baseball suit, "Sleeptite Tigers" printed on back of jacket.   1 pair blue and beige baseball stockings.   1 pair black baseball shoes.
Act I.   Scene 6.   Picnic Scene.
  Repeat as Act I, Scene 5.
Act I.   Scene 7.   Picnic Crossover.
  Repeat as Act I, Scene 5.
Act I.   Scene 10.   Factory.
  Repeat as Act I, Scene 2.
Act II.   Scene 5.   Hernando's Hideaway.
  1 dark grey 2-piece suit.   1 grey and red tie.   1 white shirt.   Repeat shoes and socks, Act I, Scene 2.
Act II.   Scene 7.   Seven-and-a-Half Cents.
  Repeat as Act I, Scene 2.
Act II.   Scene 7.   Finale.
  1 red night-gown.   Repeat shoes and socks, Act I, Scene 2.

JOE

Act I.   Scene 2.   Factory.
1 pair blue dungarees.   1 red check shirt.   1 pair fawn socks.   1 pair black shoes.

Act I.   Scene 3.   Elevator Scene.
Repeat as Act I, Scene 2.

Act I.   Scene 5.   Picnic Crossover.
1 pair brown trousers.   1 brown and gold check shirt.   1 pair blue canvas shoes.   Repeat socks, Act I, Scene 2.

Act I.   Scene 6.   Picnic Scene.
Repeat as Act I, Scene 5.

Act I.   Scene 7.   Picnic Crossover.
Repeat as Act I, Scene 5.

Act I.   Scene 10.   Factory.
Repeat as Act I, Scene 2.

Act II.   Scene 2.   Kitchen Scene.
1 light brown 2-piece suit.   1 white shirt.   1 red satin tie.   Repeat shoes and socks, Act I, Scene 2.

Act II.   Scene 6.   Office Scene.
Repeat as Act I, Scene 2.

Act II.   Scene 7.   Seven-and-a-Half Cents.
Repeat as Act I, Scene 2.

Act II.   Scene 7.   Finale.
1 pair pajamas: Trousers—Plain red.   Jacket—White with red spots.   Repeat shoes and socks, Act I, Scene 2.

SINGING AND DANCING BOYS

Various costumes to all Scenes plus pajamas for Finale.

AVERAGE OF RUNNING TIMES—3 PERFORMANCES

Overture	4 mins. 45 secs.
Prologue	1 min. 15 secs.
1st Factory	11 mins. 45 secs.
1st Hallway	5 mins. 30 secs.
1st Office	15 mins. 50 secs.
1st Picnic Crossover	4 mins. 55 secs.
Picnic Scene	14 mins. 48 secs.
2nd Picnic Crossover	4 mins. 30 secs.
1st Kitchen	7 mins. 54 secs.
2nd Hallway	4 mins. 35 secs.
2nd Factory	6 mins. 28 secs.
Interval	15 mins. 0 secs.
Entracte	3 mins. 0 secs.
Eagle Hall	6 mins. 30 secs.
2nd Kitchen	7 mins. 26 secs.
Tick Tock Scene	4 mins. 32 secs.
2nd Office	7 mins. 20 secs.
Hernando's Crossover	2 mins. 55 secs.
Hernando's Hideaway	6 mins. 25 secs.
Jealousy Ballet	5 mins. 15 secs.
Jealousy Ballet " Strip "	1 min. 15 secs.
3rd Office	5 mins. 28 secs.
Seven-and-a-Half Cents	6 mins. 55 secs.
Finale	3 mins. 0 secs.
Calls and Anthem	2 mins. 0 secs.

2 hrs. 39 mins. 16 secs.

Printed by Watkiss Studios Ltd., Biggleswade, Beds. 4/93